Pop-over
1942

Kitchen Dinner
1941
Claire McCardell

For Gabriella

For Tom —

Best
Better than you can't
Better than other American
Original!

Kohle Yohner

Claire McCardell: Redefining Modernism

by Kohle Yohannan and Nancy Nolf
Foreword by Dorothy Twining Globus
with an Introduction by Valerie Steele

Principal photography by Irving Solero

Harry N. Abrams, Inc., Publishers

Editor: Ruth A. Peltason

Editorial Assistant: Julia Gaviria

Designer: Carol A. Robson

Page 2: Hostess dress (detail).
Silk. c. 1949.
Fashion Institute of Technology.
Gift of Adrian McCardell. 76.173.1

Library of Congress Cataloging-in-Publication Data
Yohannan, Kohle.
       Claire McCardell : redefining modernism / by Kohle Yohannan and Nancy Nolf ; with an introduction
  by Valerie Steele ; foreword by Dorothy Twining Globus ; principal photography by Irving Solero.
               p.   cm.
       Includes bibliographical references and index.
       ISBN 0–8109–4375–1 (hardcover). — ISBN 0–8109–2764–0 (fit : pb)
       1. McCardell, Claire, 1905–1958. 2. Fashion designers—United States—Biography.
  3. Women fashion designers—United States—Biography. 4. Costume design—United
  States—History—20th century.   I. Title.
  TT505.M33Y64 1998
  746.9'2'092—dc21
  [B]   98–3123

Printed and bound in Japan

Harry N. Abrams, Inc.
100 Fifth Avenue
New York, N.Y. 10011
www.abramsbooks.com

Contents

Acknowledgments

This book is dedicated to the McCardell family. The authors wish to acknowledge their generous support through every stage of this project. Our special thanks to Mr. Robert C. McCardell for so many hours spent in the McCardell family home poring over documents.

The authors would like to thank the following individuals and institutions for their knowledge and expertise and their generosity in sharing it: Neely Barnwell, Geoffrey Beene, Christopher Bosch, Gail Marie Denny, Jean Dreusedow, Marie Essex, Donna Karan, Harold Koda, Al Landa, Richard Martin, Bill Rancitelli, Carol Robson, Dennita Sewell, Elaine Soares, and Pam Vassil.

Dorothy Twining Globus, Ellen Shanley, Irving Solero, Valerie Steele, and the staff at Fashion Institute of Technology, New York.

Timothy Gunn, Vera Hoar, Clinton Kuopus, Frank Rizzo, and the staff in the library at Parsons School of Design, New York.

Martha Church, Shirley Peterson, the Hood College Board of Associates, and the staff in the Beneficial-Hodson Library and the Office of Conference Services and Special Events at Hood College, Frederick, Maryland.

For their support and assistance throughout this project we would also like to thank: Julia Gaviria, Simonette Hakim, Margaret Hindman, Tav Holmes, Bruce Jolly, Peggy Larsen, Dee Dee Phillips, Lorraine Reid, Lorraine Runyon, Elaine Stainton, Andrea Valerio, Galiya Valerio, Jacques Valerio, and Melissa Yelton as well as the families of both authors.

For assistance and expertise with photography: Bengtt Carllson, Debra Cohen, Suzanne Goldstein, Brian Hetherington, Deidre Lawrence, Matthew Marden, Dianne Nilsen, Sidney Frissel Stafford, Christa Zinner, and the Staley-Wise Gallery.

Our special thanks goes to our editor, Ruth Peltason, whose unerring judgment has made a world of difference.

KOHLE YOHANNAN AND NANCY NOLF

Foreword

Claire McCardell is one of the most important American designers of the twentieth century and The Museum at the Fashion Institute of Technology has one of the world's most extensive collections of her work. Over the years, many of her fans have donated their favorite McCardells to the museum, where they are accessible to scholars and students alike. When a French television crew needed to shoot genuine McCardell clothes, FIT was the museum they contacted.

The Museum at FIT welcomes this opportunity to pay tribute to America's great designer by collaborating on this book and by organizing a concurrent exhibition. In this retrospective, over one hundred ensembles are presented, together with photographs, fashion illustrations, and related ephemera to document McCardell's career.

This project has been an enthusiastic collaboration with Kohle Yohannan of The Parsons School of Design, New York, and Nancy Nolf of Hood College, Frederick, Maryland, who have generously shared their years of research, their archival findings, and their passion for Claire McCardell. Thanks are also due to the museum staff, especially to Valerie Steele, Irving Solero, Ellen Shanley, and Fred Dennis.

More than most of the other clothes in the museum's collection, the McCardells are well worn. Often, they have altered hemlines that suggest the tendency of their devoted owners to continue wearing them for years. Even as they hang in the storeroom, these clothes reflect the philosophy of the designer:

> "Clothes ought to be useful and comfortable. I've always wondered why women's clothes have to be delicate—why they couldn't be practical and sturdy as well as feminine."

DOROTHY TWINING GLOBUS
DIRECTOR
THE MUSEUM AT THE FASHION INSTITUTE OF TECHNOLOGY
NEW YORK, NEW YORK

McCardell's American Look

By Valerie Steele

Claire McCardell was never one of my favorite designers. Unlike Balenciaga or Mme Grès, she did not make drop-dead beautiful clothes. McCardell was a realist, not an artist or an architect of fashion. Working within the parameters of the American ready-to-wear industry, she designed stylish and affordable clothes. Significantly, McCardell's clothes are always described as comfortable and practical, attributes that seem worthy but unexciting.

I can sympathize with the copywriter at *Harper's Bazaar*, who once demanded to know what was so great about a particular McCardell dress. "But, Alice, it's wonderful," replied the legendary fashion editor Diana Vreeland. "It's so pathetic." "I knew immediately what she meant," recalled the copywriter, Alice Morris. "I couldn't use the word 'pathetic,' but she was so right. It was a new frugal silhouette with that tight top so close through the shoulders."

Compared to the more lavish and formal creations of the Paris couture, McCardell's clothes were simple, frugal, humble—easy to make and easy to wear. They were not, however, necessarily easy to design; in fact, McCardell had carefully studied the work of Madeleine Vionnet, the French couturière, who was probably the greatest dressmaker of the twentieth century.

Journalists and fashion historians usually describe McCardell as the creator of "The American Look," but this kind of patriotic propaganda is too simplistic. In my book, *Women of Fashion: Twentieth-Century Designers,* I titled the chapter on McCardell (and her contemporaries) "All-American." Nonetheless, I've never been entirely comfortable with the popular perception of American style. During the 1940s, the term *the American Look* functioned primarily as a promotional tool that sold clothes by generating pride in American-made goods. Indeed, as early as 1932, Lord & Taylor began to promote the American designer movement—although the designers themselves usually remained anonymous. World War II undoubtedly helped American designers, including McCardell. Because they were cut off from French fashion by the Nazi Occupation of Paris, American manufacturers and department stores were desperate for homegrown talent.

Fashion editor Bettina Ballard recalled that American designers received "an inordinate amount of publicity, what with Paris dead to the press, and also because they represented a good national fashion story." Ballard herself disliked "the glorified covered-wagon quality" of the genre, but she recognized that it helped put Seventh Avenue on the map. After the war, however, Paris staged a spectacular comeback, and Christian Dior's "New Look" of 1947 launched a decade dominated by French fashion. Only a handful of American designers continued to maintain a high profile, among them Claire McCardell. Pioneer feminist Betty Friedan once described McCardell as "the girl who defied Dior," but it would be more accurate to say that she ignored him and continued to go her own way.

During the 1950s, the popular discourse on American fashion was characterized by Cold War rhetoric (and Paris bashing). Journalists tended to combine possibly valid insights about different national styles with an unquestioning ideological assumption that American fashion represented "freedom" and "democracy." The view of Paris as a symbol of sartorial slavery is a long-held tradition in America. Nineteenth-century dress reformers complained bitterly that the "daughters of Puritan ancestors" wore fashions that originated "in the wicked city of Paris," and they urged "all lovers of liberty . . . to free American women from the domination of foreign fashion." In the early twentieth century, the *New York Times* even launched a contest to design an American dress that would combine "patriotism, [moral] sentiment, and business." During World War II, American newspapers happily proclaimed "Paris is Dead; long live New York!"

Similarly, in 1955, *Time* magazine reported that "When [McCardell] is in Paris on vacation, she visits no collections lest she be influenced by what she sees." When I read this kind of thing, I have to ask myself, What does it mean to describe McCardell as a great American designer? Without positioning Paris as the evil Other, could we still identify an American style of dress? What role did McCardell really play in the creation of modern American sportswear? Obviously, she helped put Seventh Avenue on the map. But . . . then what?

The evidence for McCardell's significance turned out to be right in front of me—in the clothes themselves. The Museum at the Fashion Institute of Technology has one of the world's best collections of Claire McCardell's work, much of it donated by her brothers. When the muse-

Day dress. Cotton. c. late 1940s–1950. Fashion Institute of Technology. Gift of Jacqueline Weinman. 84.35.1 Women enjoyed wearing McCardell's wrap-and-tie styles, such as this plaid hostess dress, in part because the self-ties allowed them to "customize" their own natural waistline. As the designer pointed out, this made the ensemble uniquely one's own.

um's director, Dorothy Twining Globus, decided to mount a retrospective of McCardell's work, I had the opportunity of examining about three hundred of her outfits in the museum's collection. After such an analysis, I had a much better idea of her contributions to fashion. Working together with colleagues in the department of costume, a preliminary selection was made of about fifty of the most important pieces.

The principle behind our initial selection was the desire to convey the primary characteristics of McCardell's style—her design innovations, sometimes known as "McCardellisms." These include her signature metal fastenings (such as brass hooks and eyes), double rows of topstitching, spaghetti string ties, long sashes, wrap-and-tie separates, and menswear details. She had an affinity for so-called common materials, such as denim and calico, as well as the latest in high-tech performance fabrics, such as stain-proof and elasticized stretch cottons. McCardell designed a variety of different types of clothing, including day dresses, play clothes, suits, coats, evening gowns, and active sportswear—all characterized by her style of casual, easy elegance.

We also wanted to place McCardell's work within its historical context, because many of her innovations have become intrinsic to modern fashion. As early as 1936, for example, McCardell had developed a system of interchangeable separates—an idea that was literally decades ahead of its time. Indeed, part of my problem appreciating McCardell had to do with how thoroughly her ideas have been assimilated into contemporary fashion. To get an accurate sense of her impact, it was necessary for me to go back and reread magazine and newspaper articles, and even advertisements, from the 1940s and 50s.

In her time, McCardell's work was frequently characterized as "revolutionary." In 1944, for example, *Harper's Bazaar* captioned a photograph of a red tweed suit: "Right, ready and revolutionary for every girl in America . . . something of the pioneer woman in the frugal but beautiful cut of the suit . . . something of our workmen in the stout welt-seaming . . . something of Flash Gordon in the adventurous hood." After this rather exalted beginning, the copywriter turned to more prosaic information: "The suit, in Ben Mann tweed, about $50. The hood, about $8. Claire McCardell, at Lord and Taylor." This is actually the only time that the name *Claire McCardell* appears in the accompanying article, which, nevertheless, provides valuable clues about her contributions to American style.

I believe that any mention of "revolution" must have referred, at least in part, subliminally perhaps, to the Soviet Union—at the time our most powerful ally against Nazi Germany. This was, moreover, a *red* suit. Any possible anxiety about communism is assuaged by the patriotic reference to pioneer women, only to be triggered again by the reference to proletarian men. These are, however, American workmen, as can be seen by the inclusion of an advertising image of a workman in denim overalls ("long wearing extra roomy $1.47"). Inexpensive and tough, denim has long carried connotations of working-class strength and authenticity, as well as being regarded, worldwide, as an "American" material. Denim was thus a natural for McCardell's aesthetic, and she used the material often. Moreover, the text called attention to the overalls' "stitched and riveted sharpness"—qualities that also characterized McCardell's work, and not only in her affinity for visible top-stitching.

The article was illustrated with a picture of the comic book superhero Flash Gordon, together with a female counterpart, both dressed in unisex tights and hooded tunics. This futuristic style of clothing was described as being "almost abstract." With this expression, the writer moves away from references to patriotism and practicality, and toward an emphasis on cutting-edge style.

In this respect, it is also significant that McCardell's work was frequently compared to that of the dancer and choreographer Martha Graham. According to *Vogue* (January 1950), the American woman of the 1940s had "a frugal, space-silhouetted American primitive look that Martha Graham helps her to visualize, and Claire McCardell and Capezio help her to achieve." These are not, probably, the adjectives that we would use today to describe either Graham or McCardell, but they provide insight into the perceptions of an earlier era.

Similarly, in 1949 *Harper's Bazaar* described a wool jersey bicycling ensemble by McCardell as "A revolutionary outfit . . . yet a classic the day it was born." A stylistic analysis of the accompanying photograph indicates that the look was "revolutionary" because of the degree of body exposure and ease of movement. In retrospect, it was "classic," because McCardell's design philosophy made comfort look stylish. Another bicycling ensemble in the collection of The Museum at FIT has the same kind of appeal. It consists of a hooded gray wool jersey top and matching culottes. The use of culotte trousers, rather than a skirt, is obviously a functional design component that maximizes freedom of movement. The top is practical, too, being close-fitting and flexible as a sweater. The only "decoration" is a row of buttons up the left side, a use of fastenings that was typical of McCardell's work. Not only is this outfit practical, it is also graceful, because of the visual contrast between the streamlined top and flowing culottes. The hood, of

Claire McCardell in the last year of her life.
Photo. Mark Shaw. 1958

course, provides warmth and protection as needed, and folds down into a quasi-turtleneck. But the hood also has adventurous, heroic, and futuristic associations, which probably appealed equally to McCardell—and to her fans.

The theme of youth recurs repeatedly in the contemporary literature on McCardell. "For devotees of Claire McCardell . . . smart young clothes . . . young, vivacious, different," boasted an advertisement of 1952. Just as McCardell herself was often described (even in middle age) as "the typical American girl," so, too, were her clothes described as "favorites of the young-minded." They also suited those with young bodies: McCardell's clothes "make the waist look young, lithe and naturally small without squeezing." Significantly, her designs were frequently featured in magazines directed toward a younger audience, such as *Junior Bazaar* and *Mademoiselle*, indicating that a significant part of her market consisted of college students and "career girls."

One reason that so many of McCardell's designs still look fresh is that she often created for younger women. "Claire McCardell dresses will be going back to college soon," announced a newspaper article of 1944, which went on to describe McCardell as "the most youthful of the designers, and the one who creates almost exclusively for school girl figures and fancies." As designer Lee Evans said in 1972, "When I was a student, she was my inspiration. There were other designers who were important, like Adrian, but I always thought they made clothes for my mother—she made clothes for me."

McCardell was not, of course, the only designer who advocated a young and casual style of dress. As *Life* pointed out in 1946, there were several women designers, including Tina Leser and Carolyn Schnurer, whose ideal was also "the long-legged, tennis-playing, swimming girl." McCardell was certainly the most influential exponent of this style. Nevertheless, when paging through old magazines, my colleagues and I were often unable to identify, just by looking at the picture, whether a particular dress or playsuit was by McCardell or one of her competitors.

Obviously, McCardell did not single-handedly "invent" American sportswear, which had its roots in the nineteenth century—but she did contribute significantly to the rise of modern sportswear. In a 1954 article for *Sports Illustrated,* she wrote: "Sports clothes changed our lives because they changed our thinking about clothes." By giving women "freedom," sports clothes helped make them "independent." McCardell's bathing suits provide an excellent example of her innovative approach. While most bathing suits of the 1940s and 1950s had complicated underpinnings, McCardell's were unlined and unpadded. As a result they look astonishingly modern today, and they were more than a bit shocking in their time. McCardell's bathing suits were strictly "for the young and brave," declared a journalist for *Cosmopolitan* (January 1947) since it took either "a perfect figure or perfect nerve" to wear them. A typical McCardell swimsuit in the collection of The Museum at FIT is made of black wool jersey with a low V-shaped neckline, deep-cut sleeves, gilt hook-and-eye fastenings down the front, and a cord belt—all features that likewise characterized many of her dresses.

It is clear that McCardell was deeply committed to the democratization of fashion. As she once wrote, "I belong to a mass-production country where any of us, all of us, deserve the right to good fashion and where fashion must be available to all." Her famous Pop-over dress, a self-aproned, wrap-front denim dress, first made in 1941, sold for only $6.95. In 1943 *Mademoiselle* gave her a merit award for providing "flair-at-a-price." At a time when most manufacturers in the United States were content to make cheap copies of Paris fashions, McCardell combined imaginative design with attention to the requirements of mass production. In the process, she really did help put Seventh Avenue on the map and was instrumental in the creation of modern American sportswear. It is impossible to imagine a Calvin Klein or a Donna Karan or a Marc Jacobs had there not first been Claire McCardell.

Opposite:
In the late 1920s McCardell worked as a model for B. Altman's and various Seventh Avenue showrooms. Her all-American unaffected good looks, idiosyncratic stance, and unpredictable hairstyles made her immediately popular among her peers.

Far left:
At the age of 3

Near left:
Claire (center) with her brother, Adrian, and her mother. In addition to her natural athleticism, Claire's interest in clothes and design was imparted from her fashionable Southern mother.

Claire McCardell, America's most American designer, was born May 24,

Claire, at right, with Adrian and Robert McCardell. The drop-waisted cotton shift with grosgrain sash that Claire is wearing is one of the first creations crafted by Claire and the family seamstress Annie Koogle.

1905, in Frederick, Maryland, a small town in central Maryland

rich in eighteenth-century architecture and steeped in Civil War history. Claire was the oldest in her family, and had three brothers, Adrian, Robert, and John. Her father, Adrian Leroy McCardell, was a state senator and the president of the Frederick County National Bank, as was his father before him. Her mother, Eleanore Clingan McCardell, was the daughter of a Confederate officer from Jackson, Mississippi, who had met her future husband while visiting cousins in Frederick and later returned there to marry and raise a family. Gregarious and optimistic, Claire's mother was remembered by friends and family as a gracious Southern belle who was as well read and informed as she was demure and unassuming. The influence of both parents was evident in both Claire's personal character and design aesthetic: the bold, honest elegance of the well-tailored man and the spirited, unfussy femininity of an active lady of leisure.

Like many well-to-do women of her era, Eleanore McCardell retained the services of a personal dressmaker and kept abreast of international fashion news by reading American and European fashion magazines. Eleanore McCardell's avid interest in these periodicals provided Claire with her first exposure to fashionable women and the clothes they wore and later proved to be a significant factor in the course of her future career.

Frances Staley Smith, a childhood playmate of Claire's, remembers that by the time Claire was five years old, she had compiled a three-foot-high stash of her mother's discarded fashion magazines from which the two girls would cut paper dolls in the spacious attic of the McCardell's three-story Federal home. It seems that "Claire was never quite pleased with exactly what she found," and was quick to snip the sleeve of one dress, pasting it to the bodice of another, declaring with the frank confidence rarely found in adults that she was "making them better."[1] McCardell recalled the paper dolls of her childhood in a speech nearly five decades later, reminiscing that it was at that point "my eyes began their training."[2]

Claire also loved dressing up in her mother's clothes— "playing lady" she called it—while assuming the poses of the models in the fashion magazines. As an adult, the designer recalled that, "It wasn't me in the clothes, or just wearing them, that interested me—it was the clothes in relation to me—how *changed* I felt once in them."[3]

Claire at 17

From even her earliest designs, McCardell's tendency toward leisure and activewear was apparent. These watercolor sketches of McCardell playsuits most likely date from 1926, her first year at Parsons.

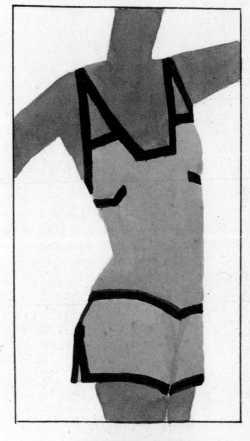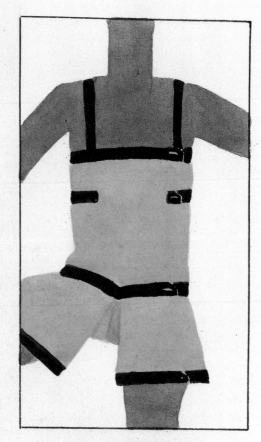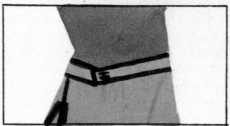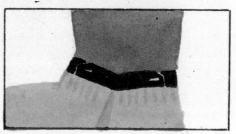

C. M°CARDELL

McCardell, at right, in her first jersey knit swimming costume. c. 1920. In later years, easy-care wool jersey would become one of the designer's trademark fabrics.

One of the earliest and most direct influences on Claire's early views about clothing was Annie Koogle, an American-born dressmaker of German descent who was employed by the McCardell family. Her visits to the McCardell home provided Claire with her first hands-on training in the design and creation of clothing. At every opportunity, the young McCardell was at Miss Koogle's side as the veteran seamstress fashioned clothing for the entire McCardell family on her treadle-step sewing machine. For the most part, Mrs. McCardell's ensembles were chosen from the pages of the *Vogue* pattern books, while others were hybrids of several designs combined to create the best effect. After preparing a sketch of the desired design, Miss Koogle would then drape, draft, cut, and adapt each garment while young Claire sat watching. This early exposure to clothing construction had a lasting influence on McCardell, who would always conceive of and design clothes with a firsthand knowledge of and respect for the techniques and production methods employed to create the final garment. This grounded understanding of body-specific clothing construction was the foundation of McCardell's commercial success. Her designs evidenced a rarely encountered sensitivity

Charcoal and watercolor rendering by Claire McCardell, c. 1927

Watercolor by Claire McCardell of a woman in a long skirt and smoking jacket, c. 1926. Growing up with three brothers, McCardell developed a lasting appreciation for the clean lines and practical aspects of menswear design.

to the female body which prompted legendary fashion editor Diana Vreeland nearly three decades later to express her unfaltering belief in the designer's skills, insisting that Claire McCardell always "knew and respected the human body and its proportions, totally, totally, TOTALLY!"[4]

Growing up with three brothers, Claire was well acquainted with the comfort and practical ease of menswear. Involved in outdoor sports from an early age, McCardell's active life-style was often better suited by a borrowed pair of her brother's trousers than by the smart drop-waisted dresses she favored on less casual occasions. By the time she was in her early teens, Claire was already dismantling her own and her brothers' clothes and remaking them for herself in much the same manner as she had approached the paper dolls—intent on "making them better." However, she occasionally met with less than ideal results: recounting the stream of missing shirts and jackets, one brother fondly remembered that his sister was "creative to the point of being unharnessable."[5] Later in life, Claire spoke with humor of her early assaults on the family wardrobe, admitting that she "didn't sew well," but that she "got an effect, you might say."[6]

McCardell's early appreciation of men's tailoring and construction details—the generous side pockets found in men's trousers, the deeper armholes in men's jackets, Levi topstitching, the use of sturdy cottons and boldly striped shirting—influenced and contributed to her design vocabulary. Ultimately, these masculine-inspired details would find their way into even the softest, most feminine McCardell designs. When teased about her childhood reputation as a tomboy (she was known as "Kick" among the neighborhood children), Claire often countered that as pretty as some clothes were they simply got in the way when trying to climb trees. Frankly disinterested in fashion's gender expectations, McCardell expressed her common-sense approach to dressing in later years by asserting that, "Men are free of the clothes problem, why shouldn't I follow their example?"[7]

In 1923, several months before graduating from Frederick High School, McCardell announced to her family her ambition to work toward a career in fashion. Despite her more forward-thinking mother's gentle interventions, Claire's plans to study fashion illustration and costume design in New York City were vetoed by her protective father, who thought she was too young to leave home. Disheartened, McCardell reluctantly spent the next two years studying home economics at Hood College, a liberal arts college for women, whose picturesque campus and Georgian-style buildings were within walking distance of the family home. More than a little discouraged, and quietly rebellious, Claire did not warm to the academic environment. She chose to major in home economics solely to get a sewing class. Though she excelled in her pattern making and costume design classes, McCardell freely admitted to having what she called "tendencies towards disaster" in her required chemistry course ("I learned that acid burns") and cooking courses ("I learned that many other things burned, too").[8]

In the spring of 1925, nearing the end of her second year at Hood, it became clear to both Claire and her professors that the academic life was not her strong suit. Determined to realize her dream to work in the fashion world, McCardell did what few small-town girls of her era would ever have dared to do: she withdrew from Hood, a college founded in part by her paternal grandfather, and with the help of her mother and against all odds, convinced her reluctant father to allow her to attend a three-year program in costume illustration and construction at the School of Fine and Applied Arts (later, the Parsons School of Design) in New York City.

Within the social context of 1925, the leap from home economics major in Frederick, Maryland, to art student in Manhattan was characteristically ambitious. That she was allowed to go says as much for the faith her parents placed in her as it does for the maverick determination which was so much a part of the McCardell personality. "Determined to save the world from ugliness and dreary clothes," as McCardell put it in a letter to a high school friend, she declined her mother's offer to send her off to New York with a new wardrobe, explaining that she couldn't possibly predict which clothes would suit a life-style that she wasn't yet living. Claire asked for a rain check and some pocket money to buy fabric and a good pair of scissors instead.

Arriving in New York City in 1926, McCardell roomed with two class-mates from Parsons, Joset Walker and Mildred Boykin (later Mildred Orrick), both of whom became successful designers in their own right. The three young women lived at the Three Arts Club on West 85th Street, a society-supported organization that hosted cultural events and community perfor-mances while providing accommodations for students pursuing careers in the arts. As well as providing job opportunities, dinner invitations, and spare theater tickets to the tenants, the wealthy members and supporters of the club hosted frequent rummage sales where they made their cast-off, gen-tly worn Paris originals available to the club's boarders for as little as five dollars apiece. Claire and her new scissors were among the elated recipients of this windfall *de luxe*. With the exception of photographs in magazines and a few of her mother's imported dresses or hats, this was McCardell's first real exposure to couture clothing by name designers. Buying as many as she could afford, McCardell promptly set about deconstructing and redesigning the luxurious garments, once again, "making them better."

McCardell soon discovered that the Three Arts Club also supported an in-house theater group with an extensive wardrobe of old costumes for use when the club's members staged small plays or hosted costumed events. Claire promptly appointed herself designer-in-residence and set about adapting and remaking costumes for the club's plays and events as well as creating outfits for herself and her roommates. Among Claire's circle of friends at the club was Gay Roddy, an aspiring young textile designer. This friendship would have a profound impact on the unfolding of McCardell's professional life: in later years, and on more than one occasion, Roddy intro-duced McCardell to key individuals who would prove to be pivotal in the evolution of her design career.

McCardell's first year of study at Parsons found her in a foundation course much like the German Bauhaus system in which incoming stu-dents were trained in the fundamental arts of rendering, sculpting, and life drawing before advancing to their chosen field of specialization. Claire was selectively attentive during this first year at Parsons, and as she had been at Hood, remained uninterested in academic life. No doubt dis-tracted by the excitement of New York City and a new life away from Frederick, McCardell finished her first two semesters with lackluster year-end evaluations. McCardell wanted to make clothes; aware that her second year of study at Parsons included classes in fashion design and construction taught in Paris, she convinced her instructor, Van Day Truex, who would be leading the group of students to Paris, that once in France her grades would improve. Truex, who later went on to become the president of Parsons and a major McCardell supporter, remembered Claire's uneven performance as a student, saying that she was "a woman with a mission."[9]

Claire as rendered in this 1927 watercolor
and charcoal study by Chester Slack,
a Parsons classmate.

Paris

In the 1920s many of the students enrolled in the Parsons fashion program
traveled abroad in their second year for two semesters of intensive study in
the midst of the great couturiers of the period. McCardell's overly protective
father, however, was apprehensive about Claire going abroad—even in a
group. Aware that her daughter's enthusiasm and excitement about living in
the French capital had played a major role in her choice of Parsons, Claire's
mother once again provided the necessary diplomatic interventions at home,
and Claire went to Paris with a generous allowance.

In the early fall of 1926, Claire McCardell arrived in the Paris of Coco
Chanel, Pablo Picasso, and Ernest Hemingway—the same Paris that fostered Jean Cocteau, immortalized American jazz, and had lured Nijinsky
and Diaghilev from the Russian front. McCardell and her classmates (including Walker and Orrick) lived and studied at Parsons's Place des Vosges
facility set within the splendid sixteenth-century square that had for four
hundred years been used by French kings for processions and royal cere-
monies. In addition to attending classes, McCardell, who had originally

intended to pursue a career as a fashion illustrator, worked part-time as an intern, tracing and copying the drawings of top designers for a firm which made such reproductions available to the international fashion trade. At the time, Claire was enrolled in a degree program called Costume Illustration and Costume Construction. Considering the extremely limited demand for designers as such, the Parsons program was the closest to a formal education in fashion an aspiring American fashion designer could obtain during that period short of on-the-job training with an established dressmaker. During the 1920s, "fashion designers" as we know them were a rarity in America, where only the most exclusive, one-of-a-kind houses or dressmaker's salons employed a designer. Otherwise, sketchers, loosely comparable to today's stylists, were hired by manufacturers to modify or otherwise "borrow" from couture designers and incorporate details into marketable—more affordable—fashions. Given the American tendency toward copying, it is easy to comprehend McCardell's early fascination with Parisian fashion and French couture, where designers such as Gabrielle (Coco) Chanel or Madeleine Vionnet (McCardell's first idol) designed with complete freedom from the moment their inspirations took form either on the sketch pad or as an original muslin, to the final cut of the fabrics that would bring their visions to life.

Especially important to Claire McCardell was Madeleine Vionnet, certainly one of the most important dressmakers of the twentieth century. McCardell's appreciation of Vionnet's innovations—especially her knowledge and deft manipulation of the bias cut—are apparent in even the earliest McCardell drawings made while she was a student in Paris. In the context of Paris fashion of the late 1920s and 1930s, Madeleine Vionnet warrants a closer look, for her imposing uniqueness and in order to form a better understanding of just what the young McCardell might have recognized of her own spirit in that of Vionnet. Viewed against the backdrop of her contemporaries, Vionnet was in many ways atypical. Despite this fact, or perhaps even because of it, McCardell was fascinated by her work, and consequently Madeleine Vionnet, more than any other designer, unwittingly contributed to the formation of the mature McCardell's design vocabulary. Vionnet's innovative construction and fabric-handling techniques, and her intimately "feminine" design influences (she had trained as a lingerie designer) emerged at times quite visibly, at others almost imperceptibly, in the work of Claire McCardell during her three decades of conscientious observation of the tastes and practical needs of American women.

Among the most visible Vionnet influences in McCardell's work are Claire's bias-cut, pieced-bodice jersey sheaths as well as her day dresses of the 1940s and 1950s, which often have a fit, fabric grain manipulation, and seam pattern surprisingly similar to Vionnet's while being quite unlike the typical American production-line dress of the period. Vionnet's flowing, streamlined sashes and bows (usually of silk), which attached at the bodice and wrapped over the shoulders and side seams,

Madeleine Vionnet halter dress from 1937.
For McCardell, Vionnet's design genius was
a longlasting influence on her own work.
Photo, Horst, c. 1937

Opposite:
Claire McCardell wearing her own silk jersey
pleated column dress. The plunging neckline and
sensitively handled fabric grain of this dress were
clearly inspired by Vionnet and Madame Grès,
the two designers McCardell most admired.
Photo, Herbert Matter, c. 1939

Madame Grès silk jersey sleeveless
column dress from 1940

Paris presents:
JERSEY

ALIX'S WHITE JERSEY—
a slender column of austere drapery,
very low cut in back.
Jewels from Mauboussin

were translated by McCardell into crisp cotton twills, flowing rayons, even cotton plaids.

As important as Vionnet had been to McCardell, Vionnet herself was aware of the influence that early mentors could have on the formation of a young designer's talent. She once referred to the time she had spent during the early years of this century working under her own mentor, Madame Gerber, at Callot Soeurs, saying, "I have made Rolls Royces, and without Madame . . . I probably would have made Fords."[10] Though awed by the glamour and tradition of Paris couture, McCardell may have instinctively suspected early on that there would be more room for Fords than Rolls Royces in the garages (or closets) of most American women, and prudently borrowed from the great French couturiers only what would speak to a working American housewife *and* to a European aristocrat. As if proving her own point, some thirty years later McCardell explained the distinctive simplicity and disciplined lack of grandeur in her proudly American designs by saying, "I am not a European princess, and my dinners are for six and not sixty. . . ."[11] The unmistakable influence of Madeleine Vionnet, along with the critical elements of the French haute couture (uncompromising construction, fabric knowledge, and stitch-accurate fit) ultimately found expression in McCardell's frankly casual, wholly American, mass-produced clothing which was made available at mid-market prices—a far cry from the formal Paris salons of Vionnet and Chanel.

Throughout the year abroad, Claire and her more adventurous classmates, Walker and Orrick, regularly pooled their money to acquire clothes from the Paris flea markets, as well as at sample sales held by the couture houses to which Parsons students were invited at the end of each season. True to her nature, and recalling the times as a girl when she reassembled clothes for her paper dolls, McCardell eagerly unstitched nearly every piece of clothing she acquired—disassembling the most luxurious gowns, careful always to sew them back together flawlessly after having seduced the secrets of construction from the dismantled garments. Much like the time she had spent at the side of the family seamstress, McCardell was learning—from the inside out—the methods of precision sewing employed by the great couturiers of the period. In an interview nearly two decades later, McCardell reminisced about her days as a student in Paris. Asked about her peculiar, deconstructive approach to fashion design, she explained that she "was learning important things—the way clothes worked, the way they felt, where they fastened."[12] She even seemed rather surprised that the image of a young girl dissecting a floor-length Vionnet gown with a seam ripper might elicit a shiver from the young fashion journalist seated across from her.

One "find" in particular became a bone of contention among the three enterprising fashion investors—a knee-length, black wool evening coat from the house of Jean Patou. Modeled on the strict, dapper officer's uniforms of the French *gendarmes*, its distinctive feature was a swirling cape lined in bright red wool crepe which attached at the neck and collar seams. Despite less than gentle disapproval from Walker—she called it "that *awful* thing"—

McCardell and Orrick bought it on their own and Orrick later recalled that Claire wore the coat everywhere—day and night. Claire insisted that the coat and its cape "did something—they worked." [13] Indeed, having proved itself, that "awful thing" showed up in an updated version almost twenty years later in the Townley Frocks fall line, designed by Claire McCardell. A second version, with its waist nipped in and the cape split in two, was featured in an editorial spread as well as in several advertisements in *Harper's Bazaar* in the early 1950s. Perhaps inspired by this early purchase, tie-around, shawl-attached, caped, and hooded styles were to make frequent appearances in McCardell collections in the decades that followed. On file in the United States Patent Office is an application by Claire McCardell, including a drawing and written description, for a hood McCardell had fashioned from a semi-circular, full-backed cape not so very unlike the Patou cape.

Always asking the question, "What does it do?" followed closely by "Why is it there?" McCardell conceived of clothes as objects that should function. Her design philosophies were actually more in synch with the form-follows-function principles of early industrial design than with the overtly decorative conceptions of early- to mid-twentieth-century fashion design. (When *Life* magazine ran a feature issue in 1990 chronicling the one hundred most influential Americans of the twentieth century, Claire McCardell was placed on the same page as industrial designer Raymond Loewy.)

Although Paris fashion continued to dominate both the tastes and spending habits of America in the 1920s, Claire McCardell, who was among the cheering crowd on the night that Lindbergh landed in the French capital, returned to America with an enriched understanding of European design along with a firm grasp of what styles were best left on foreign shores. With a keen respect for the refinement and construction techniques of the fashion capital's grand couture houses, McCardell made use of her French training in the formulation and development of her uniquely American style over the next thirty years.

New York Shuffle

When McCardell returned to America in the summer of 1927, she made a brief visit to Maryland, where she was greeted with the news that a letter home about the Lindbergh landing had earned her the first of what would become a lifetime of feature articles in the local paper. Pleased to see her family after such a long time away, Claire spent several days fishing with her brothers and dazzling friends and family with her stories of Paris. Once back in Manhattan, along with Walker and Orrick, McCardell secured accommodations for the coming school term and moved back to the Three Arts Club for her senior year at Parsons. Soon after the new school year began, another unimpressive report card arrived from the Paris program, and midway through the semester in New York, Claire's grades went from bad to worse. By this time McCardell's interest and attention had long since strayed from the academic arena, but despite her impatience with school she was determined to graduate and promised her mother and father in a letter written in November of 1927 that not only would she complete her degree program and get her diploma, she would improve her grades along the way. Most of this came to pass and in the spring of 1928, Claire and her classmates received their degrees from Parsons and the independent-minded designer, diploma in hand, at long last was ready to break into the fashion industry.

In order to cut living expenses, Claire shared a small apartment in midtown Manhattan with Mildred Orrick and her mother for a short period immediately after graduation. Both girls were avidly seeking work within the fashion industry but it was Orrick who first landed a position as the girl Friday for Natacha Rambova, who was establishing an exotic dress and specialty shop on East Fifty-second Street. Having enjoyed a successful career in Hollywood as a production and costume designer, Rambova's career had been temporarily bolstered by a much publicized (but not so successful) marriage to screen idol Rudolph Valentino. Despite Orrick's good fortune, McCardell, by then twenty-three years old, was not meeting with similar success. Determined to work in the fashion industry, Claire hit the streets on a door-to-door job hunt of Seventh Avenue, the heart of Manhattan's garment center, but was greeted with closed doors and icy receptionists. Determination alone (and, worse yet, inexperience) proved to be of little help in a flat economy, and despite more than two months of answering advertisements, cold calling, and interviewing, McCardell came up short and was unable to find a job.

The first of what would prove to be many short-term McCardell endeavors came in response to a want ad in *Women's Wear Daily* seeking "artistic individuals." Claire applied for the job and was hired. However, after her exposure to the glamorous world of Parisian haute couture, painting floral decoration onto paper lamp shades was not in the running for a McCardell career. Claire lasted two months before telling her mother in a letter that she wanted to dress women, not lightbulbs. At this point McCardell was back to reading the want ads and promptly responded to yet another notice placed by a wholesale house seeking a sample hand in their Seventh Avenue production room. Excited and confident, Claire prepared herself to interview for a job which she hoped would be her first major break. As it happened, however, McCardell's first professional experience in New York fashion was more like a walk-on part in a bad vaudeville skit. Inexperienced, but willing to learn, Claire liberally embellished upon her actual work experience during the interview and was delighted when she was hired on the spot as the second pattern cutter in a typically manic "have it done yesterday" Seventh Avenue workroom. She quickly learned, however, that the pace and expectations of the New York garment industry were a far cry from the patient, nurturing environment of the Parsons classrooms. McCardell was interviewed, hired, began work, and was fired all within seven hours. As the designer later remembered it, "It was a one-day disaster!"[14]

During these frustrating first months after graduation from Parsons, letters from McCardell to her mother were replete with her mounting exasperation. Discouraged by what seemed to be an endless stream of "nos," Claire's health took a turn for the worse, and with a near case of pneumonia, she was persuaded by her mother to return home to Frederick for a short time during the winter of 1928 to recoup and rethink her career strategy.

Once home, Claire's protective father, seeing his only daughter in what would prove to be her hardest of times (and, rather surprisingly, still convinced that Claire was "too young to leave home") tried persuading her to remain in Frederick and even suggested that she take "a sensible position" as a local schoolteacher.[15] Perhaps it was this suggestion that restored Claire's health and her New York restlessness, for she returned to Manhattan inside of a week, more determined than ever to make her mark, this time armed with a small allowance from her parents to help smooth the road along the way.

Back in New York and newly settled in a room all her own in what McCardell fondly remembered as a "wonderfully less than wonderful" boardinghouse, the designer got her first significant break: in late 1928, McCardell applied and was hired as a fit model in the French Room at B. Altman's department store.[16] At the time, Altman's was one of the East Coast's most prestigious retailers of Paris couture and one-of-a-kind imports. Though low paying (her salary was twenty dollars a week), this new position provided the aspiring designer with access to the inner circle of New York's fashion cartel.

McCardell as a model, standing five feet seven inches tall, with blonde, all-American good looks, was nonetheless prone to a casual, sporty, almost lumbering gait and a slightly slouching stance—both of which were at distinct odds with the prancing, pirouetting mannequins of her day. In her later years, the designer actually trained her own showroom models to adapt this idiosyncratic, seemingly carefree posture—hands in their pockets, hips thrust forward. Claire's long, center-parted braids were another McCardell trademark which, when not swept up in a chignon, were often tucked into her collar, or worn in a continuous loop braided under her neck.

Good-looking and polite, Claire soon became known to the fashion buyers and saleswomen at Altman's, and was often asked by other store buyers and wholesalers to work in their showrooms when they needed extra girls to fill in. Though she was far more interested in the design and production of the highly sought-after imports that she was being hired to model or sell, McCardell nevertheless made eager use of these odd jobs to round out both her living expenses and her knowledge of the fashion industry while waiting for her chance to step up to the dress form.

In later years Claire always insisted with a modest laugh that she was sure that she had been "a bum model," and jested that she had merely been "on spy duty," observing and memorizing the various details and signature construction techniques of every dress that came her way.[17] In 1955, addressing a class of graduating designers at Parsons nearly twenty-five years after those first sashays through the Seventh Avenue showrooms and dress salons, McCardell strongly suggested that aspiring fashion designers would do well to garner even the smallest amount of experience modeling, knowing firsthand that it afforded the invaluable experience of actually seeing, touching, and wearing clothes from the best names in the industry. "One learns the way clothes work, where they fasten," she told the future designers, offering them the same explanation she had once given when asked about her curious passion for disassembling couture garments.[18] Clearly, a McCardell philosophy, and one born of experience, was in the making.

In late 1929, McCardell left B. Altman's when Parsons found her a job as an assistant to Emmet Joyce, who had opened his own exclusive, made-to-order salon on Fifth Avenue the year before. At the time, Joyce's dresses and ensembles were generally quite colorful, prone to applied decoration, and extremely expensive. Although she was not hired to create the line, McCardell was grateful for the inroad back to the cutting room. Working as a behind-the-scenes sketcher and saleswoman for Joyce (who had previously worked as a designer for fashion entrepreneur Hattie Carnegie), Claire remembered being pleased that "At last I had a job working with clothes, even if I wasn't designing."[19] In addition to sketching and selling, McCardell was sent out to shop the stores for "good numbers" to copy. "I hated this," she frankly admitted later in her life, "and often came back with collections of my own ideas, which I presented to my boss as rare finds from Bergdorf Goodman!"[20] Maybe he caught on, or maybe he liked her "originals," but the real surprise in store for Emmet Joyce was that his shy but remarkably talented new assistant was about to walk right out of his high-priced doors as quickly as she had just walked through them. McCardell had been with Joyce for only three months when Gay Roddy, her friend from the days of costume makeovers at the Three Arts Club, brought McCardell to Goldlac to meet knitwear manufacturer Sol Pollack, who, McCardell later said, was "quite impressed with my job with such an expensive dress house!"[21] As it happened, Pollack made McCardell an impressive offer, and so she left Emmet Joyce on good, if abrupt, terms to become Pollack's assistant at forty-five dollars a week—more than twice her previous salary.

In truth, McCardell knew little about knitwear design and manufacturing, but her days at Parsons (combined with her instinctive ability to learn quickly) made it possible for Claire to disguise this fact for a few months while she tried to learn the fundamentals of Pollack's business. In spite of her efforts, however, about six months into her new job (which again included shopping the stores for "good numbers" to copy), McCardell's new boss began to rightfully suspect that she really didn't know very much about knitwear design. To make matters worse, Pollack proved to be considerably less enthralled by her "rare finds from

Bergdorf Goodman" than her previous employer had been. At the end of eight months Pollack fired her. Specifically, he told Claire in front of a showroom full of clients and employees that she didn't understand design and should stop trying to make clothes to please herself!

Ironically, this self-referencing aspect of McCardell's approach to designing clothes made it possible for her to accomplish such a determined departure from the current norms in women's fashion. As if in response to Pollack's indelicate criticism, in later life, Claire McCardell came to be celebrated as the designer who "designs as she pleases"; indeed, she often attributed her success to the fact that she had designed things she needed for herself, adding modestly that "it just turns out that other people need them, too."[22]

In 1929, shortly after she had been fired by Pollack, Claire was working as a model for ready-to-wear designer Charlie Armour when Gay Roddy once again helped to maneuver her back behind the dress form. This time, Roddy introduced her to Robert Turk, an independent designer and dress-maker, who was preparing to place an ad in *Women's Wear Daily* seeking a design assistant. Though McCardell did not have the two requisite years of experience that Turk wanted, he must have recognized in McCardell a certain eagerness because he hired her anyway. During her time with Turk, whom Claire once described as someone who "had a way of making you do things," Claire sketched, shopped for buttons, even did some designing— anything that needed to get done. The one thing she didn't do was "sweep the floors," adding, "I can't remember why!"[23, 24]

McCardell worked alongside Turk and his private clientele for almost two full years, at which point his business began to flounder and his financial backers contemplated a merger with a larger firm. Holding out as long as possible, Turk eventually agreed to his business being absorbed by Townley Frocks, a mid-market dress and sportswear manufacturer located at 550 Seventh Avenue, which at the time was owned and operated by Henry Geiss. Robert Turk agreed to take up his new post as chief designer at Townley Frocks with just one provision: that he could bring his assistant, Claire McCardell, along with him.

In the spring of 1932, an unexpected tragedy landed McCardell in an awkward but advantageous position when Robert Turk was drowned in a boating accident over Memorial Day weekend. Townley's owner, Henry Geiss, motivated in part by faith in Claire's work and perhaps more by production deadlines, allowed McCardell, then barely twenty-seven, to complete the fall line. The finished collection was not a purely McCardell group of clothes by any measure (one dress was cut from red lamé), nor did it wow Seventh Avenue, however it was reasonably well received and the buyers placed orders. Many of the ensembles already showed clear evidence of scattered, but recognizable "McCardellisms" in their embryo stage: plaids, mitered stripes, and an awareness of the bias cut as well as several designs featuring asymmetrical closures and wrap-and-tie waists. On the strength of the first collection, Claire, who was extremely popular among the men and the women in the workrooms, was promoted by Geiss to full designer status.

Along with the high pressure demands of McCardell's new job came a few built-in perks. In keeping with the American rage for French fashion, most mid- and upper-market designers were expected to take semiannual trips to Paris to review the collections, buy samples, and as always, sketch "good numbers."

By the age of 27, Claire was blessed with great looks and an innate self-confidence.

Claire with her friend Joset Walker on deck
en route to Paris in the mid-1930s.

Portrait of Emilie Högqvist by Nordgren,
1837. Nordiska Museet

Opposite:
Revised and remade for a more contemporary feminine
American look, McCardell's puffed sleeve floral dress was
clearly adapted from historical dress of the early 19th century,
shown at left. Photo, Louise Dahl-Wolfe for *Harper's Bazaar*,
1950. Center for Creative Photography, University of Arizona

Claire often attended the seasonal showings in Paris accompanied by Joset Walker, her schoolmate from Parsons, who at the time was working on Seventh Avenue designing a line for David Goodstein, a smart but conservative dress house that turned out Paris-inspired day dresses and separates. While abroad, McCardell and Walker (who was French born and fluent in French) often made time to visit other European cities, including London and areas in the south of France and Italy. Although she had been dispatched to copy current fashions during these trips, McCardell paid more attention to the styles and basic trends of the countries she visited than to exact detailed copying of any particular garments. There are, however, a few specific examples of ideas that Claire imported during her first years at Townley which, with varying degrees of accuracy, can be traced to specific places or periods. One, mentioned by Sally Kirkland in *American Fashion*, was the dirndl skirt, which had enchanted McCardell in the mid-1930s when she was visiting Austria. Free-flowing and comfortable by design, it was a McCardell natural and was bound to catch the eye of the observant American style maker. Two years after Claire had shown it, the dirndl skirt was still enjoying enormous popularity throughout America.

On another trip to several European cites in the late 1930s, McCardell filled two shoe boxes to the brim with colored glass and crystal beads from a flea market near Budapest. Once home, she had them strung in single-color strands

and wore them by the handfuls, roped around her collarless cotton and linen dresses. The models in the McCardell showroom that season were similarly adorned with the same beads strung longer as three-stranded belts, making for smart, sleek, waist-emphasizing notes. Never one to stitch beaded or jeweled detailing directly onto a dress, McCardell instead preferred the lively use of mixed chains, beads, and metal "trinkets," as she liked to call them.

Claire's unaffected fashion-is-where-you-find-it approach to dressing often yielded some wonderful results. Her fascination with the metal fastenings and leather-yoked buckle closures often found on semi-professional European ski equipment and downhill racing clothes of the 1930s and 1940s became a McCardell staple. Beginning in the late 1930s, these large-scale clips and buckles eventually found their way onto countless McCardell outerwear designs. Scaled-down versions showed up on jackets and coats in her collections throughout her career.

In addition to the compulsory "good numbers," McCardell would return from her early scouting trips to Europe with more than just sketches. She cleverly reinterpreted Europe's contemporary street looks as well as details from historic, traditional European costumes, all of which contributed to the casually elegant, wholly American clothing the name Claire McCardell would come to represent.

McCardell's interchangeable separates systems were originally offered to buyers in the early 1930s. Sophisticated enough to go from office to opera, this forward-looking system of dressing offered working women style and versatility at an affordable price. Courtesy *Vogue*, 1945

LEFT: UNCLUTTERED WOOL JERSEY
BLOUSE, $11. RAYON-AND-
COTTON FAILLE SKIRT, $14.
RIGHT: EVENING SWEATER; RAYON
SATIN SKIRT BY CLAIRE MC CARDELL,
$55. LORD AND TAYLOR. PLATINUM,
DIAMOND JEWEL: NEIMAN-MARCUS.
● INTERIOR DESIGN: ROBSJOHN-GIBBINGS.

Even though her cinch leather belts were anywhere from 3 to 7 inches deep, they were nevertheless comfortable, yielding to the body's contours. Photo, Louise Dahl-Wolfe, 1938. Center for Creative Photography, University of Arizona

Although McCardell was inspired by these trips, she wondered why American design firms would pay their own salaried designers to travel to Paris to execute slavish copies of French fashion. Nevertheless, she knew what was expected of her and since she couldn't exert her own aesthetic autonomy over Townley's collections, McCardell remembered doing "what everybody else did in those days—copied Paris."[1] Also around this time, many of the designer's most influential design concepts were first introduced and later developed in the early 1940s: her revolutionary separates system of dressing, dresses of men's tie and muffler silk, as well as her highly improbable evening coats made from men's tweeds and wool suiting, to name but a few. It was also during these early years that some of the construction techniques and characteristic closures and details that Claire later termed her "McCardellisms" were introduced: wrap waists, sashes, spaghetti ties, and Claire's favorite brass hook-and-eye corset closures—in short, anything distinctly her own.

Claire was rarely satisfied with the standard fare offered by fabric salesmen who visited the Townley showroom and often traveled to the fabric mills in the South to see if something more to her liking could be custom-made, if it was not already available. Looking to distinguish her line from her competitors', McCardell actively combed the marketplace for unusual, experimental fabrics and suppliers of offbeat notions and fastenings. Willing to give new products a chance, Claire was one of the first designers to promote a new leather processing technology known at the time as elasticizing. The inventor, Alexander Hysa, had wandered into McCardell's office with his first sample of the cinch belt in his hands. In the hands of Claire McCardell, the cinch belt went on to become an enormously popular fad in the mid- to late 1930s. Hysa's own company, the King Fashionable Belt Company, rewarded McCardell for her assistance in promoting their product in the years that followed by creating McCardell's custom accessories at a price that would allow the designer to include an original McCardell leather belt (often as wide as seven inches) with her dresses for not much more than the plain self-fabric standards her competitors offered.

During her first few years at Townley, McCardell reluctantly gave in to the pressure to imitate Paris, but it was not without frequent flare-ups with Henry Geiss and his sales representatives. By the late 1930s, she was waging full war against the use of shoulder pads in her clothes—even her silhouettes. Made popular by Schiaparelli in the mid-1930s, padded shoulders gave the illusion of a more dramatically slender waist, but McCardell found them overly theatrical and felt that they restricted the natural movements of the body. Buyers wanted shoulder pads, however, and Geiss saw to it that they got them. McCardell herself, though, had a strong aversion to form-altering designs and opted instead for dropped shoulders and dolman sleeves despite the lasting popularity that the more severe Schiaparelli silhouette enjoyed. Though McCardell willingly acknowledged a debt to Paris for her education and understanding of garment construction, whenever possible she steadfastly resisted French influence over American fashion.

On one of her frequent trips home to visit her family in Frederick, Claire once commented to a younger brother that she could never understand why some of the prettiest women in New York walked down Fifth Avenue dressed for the Champs-Elysées.[2] McCardell knew that American women led quite different lives from their European counterparts and truly believed that only an American designer could offer them a truly *American* style. From her earliest days as a designer, McCardell was actively formulating and promoting the pared-down, no-nonsense aesthetic she felt was already an inherent part of American culture. Despite her enthusiasm, however, at nearly every juncture of her career the avant-garde visionary often encountered a gap between what she saw as "style" and what the market-place promoted as "fashion." In 1938, however, that gap began to close.

The Monastic Dress

In the fall of 1938, Townley's new talent scored her first big hit with the Monastic dress—an unfitted, waistless shift cut on the bias, which hung straight from the shoulders and was belted any way the wearer chose. The versatility and defiantly innovative nature of the design was unprecedented and purely McCardell. Despite rumors that the Monastic dress was a sleeper rescued from the rejects rack, the dress was actually a McCardell original in the purest sense of the word—something Claire had sewn for herself at home to wear as a costume for a Beaux Arts Ball in 1937. Based loosely on a traditional Algerian garment, the very first version of this dress, as re-membered by a family member, was made from gaily colored cotton batik. The easily made frontless and backless design amused Claire with its casual, flowing lines, so she and Mildred made up a version for herself in red slubbed wool to wear at the office and around town. On a day like any other, Claire was wearing the red wool dress at the office when she nearly knocked down a buyer from Best & Co. near the coffee stand. In this less than legendary way, the Monastic dress was "discovered" by the buyer who bought very little that day except for Claire's own dress, which she wanted as an exclusive for Best & Co.[3] True to her claim that she really did design first for herself, McCardell handed over the hand-sewn garment, explain-ing that she and her roommate had quickly assembled it and that it was not ready to be seen by buyers. Despite McCardell's protestations, the buyer placed an order for 100 more just like it. The Monastic dress—truly a McCardell "original"—went on to change the face of American fashion.

The Monastic dress (originally named the Nada Frock by the adver-tising department at Best & Co.) was never intended to be part of Townley's 1938 fall collection, but it became an instant hit nonetheless. Best & Co. had such an overwhelming response to the full-page advertisement that ran in the *New York Times* Sunday edition that the dress sold out within twenty-four hours. The next morning they doubled their order, yet they literally could not keep the dress in the store—dresses were sold as quickly as they were delivered. After its second sellout, the Monastic dress also became available in a floor-length evening version and was also available in slinky crepe as well as in the original lightweight wool. Rather astonishingly, the Monastic was even being presold on deposit—a retail procedure normally reserved for the limited number of expensive copies to be made from an original couture model, but a truly unprecedented response to a thirty dollar, ready-to-wear dress by a relatively unknown American designer.

When launched in 1938, McCardell's Monastic dress was revolutionary—and successful. Frontless, backless, and with no sewn-in waistline, the versatility and simplicity of the Monastic dress allowed the wearer free to wear it loose or belt it at her own discretion.

Immediately, the Monastic dress put Claire McCardell on the map, and in varying forms the free-flowing, unrestricted design would remain part of McCardell's repertoire for the duration of her career. While Seventh Avenue was still talking about Claire McCardell of Townley Frocks and her sellout Monastic dress, the designer, who was planning to submit a design under her own name for a competition at the upcoming New York World's Fair, approached Geiss with the idea of putting her own name on the Townley label. Geiss wouldn't hear of it, and though McCardell went on to take first prize at the Fair in 1939, this was one of several incidents that contributed to the strained relationship between Geiss and McCardell.[4] The second, rather surprisingly, was the Monastic dress.

Despite the success of the Monastic dress, perhaps even because of it, Geiss was nearly ruined financially from battling over copyrights against design houses and retailers who were knocking it off. Ironically, the very man who found McCardell's free-thinking design concepts so suspect in the beginning was now fighting to defend against the very same counterfeiting he had so zealously perpetrated in the past. Notwithstanding Geiss's efforts, copies of the Monastic dress soon were filling the stores faster than Townley could produce the originals. And though Geiss had strongly suggested that McCardell abandon the free-flowing silhouette in her next collection, Claire was confident that the Monastic was a proven winner and, despite abundant copies, saw a place for it in the coming season's collection. This disagreement, along with Geiss's refusal to grant McCardell's request to design under her own name, led the designer to consider working with another manufacturer. Worse yet, the legal fees and time spent haggling over the Monastic dress with copyright attorneys and the Fashion Originators Guild (an organization which attempted to curtail such infringements) had so exhausted Geiss that his health, as well as his financial backing, began to fail him, forcing Townley Frocks to close its doors in 1938. It also left America's first fashion revolutionary on the front line without a job.

Almost immediately after leaving Townley in 1938, Claire was asked to work for Hattie Carnegie, who at the time was dressing some of New York's chicest society women as well as many stage and screen stars of the period. A shrewd businesswoman, Carnegie was well aware of Townley's maverick designer and promptly intercepted McCardell before she had even begun to look elsewhere. Hattie Carnegie was a keen purveyor of taste, and though not an innovator herself, she had the uncanny ability to take the best styles of Paris and make her own rather expensive adaptations with a distinctly American feel. Her designers, among them Norman Norell and Travis Banton, created dresses based on the couture models Carnegie purchased each season on buying trips abroad—combining a collar from one, a sleeve from another, a skirt from a third. Enterprising and willing to take risks, Carnegie had great faith in Claire McCardell's work and hired her along with most of her Townley workroom to design for her private clients and also to create a line of casual but expensive clothes

called "Workshop Originals." As it turned out, however, Claire's pared-down, unfussy "Workshop" styles did not sufficiently enthrall Carnegie's high-styled patrons, who had long become accustomed to getting more glamour for their money.

A definitive early example of McCardell's casual, relaxed elegance is a brown-and-ivory striped rayon wrap-waisted dress that McCardell designed while working for Carnegie in 1939, which today is in the collection of the Costume Institute at the Metropolitan Museum of Art, New York. The flowing side-wrapping sashes reflect McCardell's lifelong admiration for Madeleine Vionnet but, despite its obvious appeal, the dress was probably not lavish enough for the majority of Carnegie's rich uptown clientele. One satisfied customer, however, was Diana Vreeland, the legendary fashion editor, who at the time was working at *Harper's Bazaar*. According to Sally Kirkland, Vreeland brought Hattie Carnegie some French jersey in 1938 and asked for "a little two-piece Chanel kind of uniform. She got a one-piece McCardell instead" and liked it so much that she asked to meet the designer.[5] Vreeland became an enthusiastic supporter of McCardell, and one of Claire's most powerful allies.

McCardell designed this brown-and-ivory
striped dress while working for Hattie Carnegie.
Photo 1939, courtesy *Vogue*

Surviving sketches from the first few months of McCardell's tenure with Carnegie show quite a few dresses which can only be described as McCardells dressed up in expensive Hattie Carnegie fabrics. Claire's sketching techniques, however, clearly and rather humorously reflected her move uptown: those from her Townley days are headless, quickly recorded lines that capture the shape and dynamic of the garment—its essential feel and little else—while those done for Carnegie not only have heads and hands, but are often fully drawn, haughty women in rather grand poses one might rightly imagine that a Hattie Carnegie customer (if not Miss Carnegie herself) might assume. Amused by this sudden upgrade in her clientele, Claire occasionally wrote the names of the most prominent Carnegie customers who had ordered her dresses on the back of her sketches. Some of these she even reported to her mother in letters sent home to the family. Rather surprisingly, Barbara Hutton, the American heiress who was dressed by the most exclusive and expensive couturiers in the world, purchased more than a few of Claire McCardell's designs. Less pleased, however, was stage star Gertrude Lawrence, who in 1939 refused a characteristically simple McCardell design for her starring role in *Skylark*, opting instead for a white beaded Norell that Miss Carnegie had quickly dispatched to appease the temperamental English actress.[6] In addition to dresses, the first pages of McCardell's notebooks from her days with Carnegie open with a section labeled "Hats for Hattie," a group of McCardell-designed millinery confections which, though sparse on details, were high on style. Most are rather severe, close-fitting, angular felt hats, more Robin Hood than Schiaparelli, although the influence of the great Italian designer is readily apparent. McCardell herself, who maintained a lifelong penchant for hats and owned literally hundreds, often said that she never saw any reason to get rid of even one.

In keeping with the leanings of Carnegie's personal tastes and clientele, McCardell was expected to maintain familiarity with French fashion news and traveled to Paris to view the collections. By 1940, however, World War II had steadily taken its toll on France's commercial infrastructure, and though unaware of it at the time, those American designers and stylists who attended the couture collections that year (McCardell among them) were unwittingly viewing the last full showings Paris would offer for the next four years. For McCardell, this trip to sketch the Paris collections for Carnegie turned out to be her last visit ever to the formal French salons. Later in her life, McCardell said that she preferred not to see the French collections for fear that they might influence her designs. Sketches from the last few months of McCardell's tenure at Hattie Carnegie do indeed indicate a reluctant nod to the French influence that Carnegie's wealthy patrons demanded, but there is also a general hesitation to embellish and a strictness of line that remain undeniably McCardell.

During the late 1930s, the independent designer was about to yield to yet another kind of influence that she had hitherto managed to resist: on board a luxury liner crossing the Atlantic, Claire met Irving Drought Harris, a handsome American architect who became her first long-standing, serious suitor and eventual husband. Harris was a distinguished-looking, large-framed man from Texas with a taste for sailing, fox hunting, and blue-blood society. However, with two young children of his own and a much publicized divorce in the air, Claire rightly suspected that Harris was bound to be a hard sell to her highly protective and religiously observant father back in Frederick. As a result, Harris and the McCardell family did not meet immediately. From the couple's very first meeting, Irving Harris and Claire McCardell began a courtship that throughout the early 1940s seemed to all who knew them to be headed well into each other's futures. They had their differences though, one of which was Harris's mercurial temperament, which had landed his first marriage on the rocks just shortly before he met Claire.

Where McCardell was shy and reserved Harris was outgoing and socially ambitious—not an uncommon dynamic as couples go and with the expected results: Claire began attending far more gala events, theater functions, and uptown charity dinners than she might have otherwise preferred. This highly visible New York nightlife, which really was not in keeping with McCardell's introverted nature, was later offset by weekend and holiday visits to a small secluded farmhouse in Frenchtown, New Jersey, which McCardell and Harris had acquired together within a few years of meeting. Without a telephone or central heat, and only a hand pump for water, this rustic retreat was exactly the quiet haven McCardell had craved since her career had begun to make more and more demands on her time.

Hattie Carnegie was well aware that Claire McCardell was a talent with which to be reckoned, but as her business and McCardell's talents were not proving mutually beneficial, she and Claire eventually conceded that they had incompatible philosophies about fashion and that an amicable parting was the only solution. According to Claire's brother, Adrian McCardell, there may have been another reason: McCardell was still not being credited for her designs.[7] After nearly two years of attempting to convince Miss Carnegie that she should be credited, and after receiving more than one imperious refusal, McCardell was again ready to move on. She left Hattie Carnegie with a clearer perception of her own design talents and the kind of women she wanted to dress.

In the summer and fall of 1940, after leaving Hattie Carnegie, Claire worked for a low-priced manufacturer called Win-Sum. Back on familiar ground (Win-Sum was located in 550 Seventh Avenue, the same building where Townley Frocks had been), McCardell may have been contemplating her next career move. But she could never have anticipated the surprise that was in store for her.

Claire McCardell Clothes

One day in the fall of 1940, McCardell found herself sharing an

elevator with Henry Geiss (the former owner of Townley Frocks), Harry Friedman (Townley's production man), and Adolph Klein, then unknown to Claire. Klein was a suave and savvy young Brooklynite who had gained a name on Seventh Avenue as a shrewd and forward-thinking salesman. Always aware of ripples in the market, Klein had followed McCardell's early career from a distance and felt certain that he recognized in the young woman the spirit of an innovator. Surprised to learn that Geiss was planning to reopen Townley under Klein's ownership, Claire expressed her sincere wishes to all present for the success of their new undertaking, and even hugged Geiss in a daughterly farewell to former tensions. Before the elevator doors had opened, however, McCardell was asked by Klein if she would consider coming back to her old job as head designer at Townley. She was dumbfounded. She had been rumored to have nearly bankrupted Geiss with her so-called unruly, outlandish designs. Speaking in later years of that on-the-spot decision that proved to have truly monumental impact on American fashion and popular culture at large, Klein underplayed his role in the coup, "In this business, you have to be exciting or basic. I figured we were too small to be basic, so we had to be exciting."[1]

As confident as Adolph Klein was in his choice, Henry Geiss had experienced McCardell's unpredictable past performance. Before agreeing to sign McCardell to a contract with the new Townley, Geiss persuaded Klein to find out from Win-Sum, Claire's current employer, how the designer's recent work was faring in the marketplace. That done, and having been told flat out "better to throw your money out the window," Geiss remained less than enthusiastic and insisted on at least one more reference—this time, a good one. Again Adolph Klein agreed, but as time was of the essence in

Day dress. Wool. 1949.
Fashion Institute of Technology.
Gift of Hood College. 96.61.14

Claire in her man-tailored tweeds on board a steamer in the late 1930s. Although McCardell had been wearing men's suiting, camel's hair, and overcoat tweeds long before heavy woolens had become acceptable in women's apparel, it took retailers more than a decade to catch on to these fabrics.

order to meet manufacturing deadlines for the upcoming season, and as he was certain that McCardell was the right choice, Klein hired Claire without waiting for the second report. When it came, Klein wasted no time sharing with Geiss a letter that arrived at his home from an East Coast retailer stating plainly, in bold print, "If I were you, I'd go shoot craps with the money. It's not as much of a gamble as Claire McCardell."[2] Even Klein characterized Claire as a twenty-to-one shot and later said that he had hired her on the strength of her Monastic dress and because he found her honesty and lack of pretension intriguing.[3] But risky or not, McCardell was a gamble Klein was willing to take and soon the buzz on Seventh Avenue was that Claire McCardell was returning to Townley Frocks. McCardell, however, made sure she returned with some new ground rules.

McCardell was indeed grateful to have been offered her job back at Townley, but excerpts from the designer's original desk notes clearly illustrate how she wanted her new role at Townley Frocks to take shape. One in particular indicates that after a few years of Seventh Avenue experience under her belt, Claire had come to possess a determination and authority rarely found in any but the most seasoned and successful fashion veterans: on the back of a phone message from 1940, Claire had penned and underlined the following "ordinance" pending her return to Townley: "Claire McCardell Clothes will all carry a C McC label—they will be produced *as the sample is made*—If you do not like the way it's made—Buy something you do like—no changes."[4] The usually soft-spoken designer was beginning to make her voice heard. McCardell returned to Townley with a long wish list, most of which was accepted, along with the help of Adolph Klein, who it seemed would do just about anything to keep his designer happy. Within six months, Klein had McCardell's name put on the label and Claire McCardell Clothes by Townley replaced the less modern Townley Frocks. Klein once revealed in an interview that Townley's business manager, Geiss (who had refused to grant McCardell this request in the past), had worried that McCardell would become too demanding if her own name was on the label instead of Townley's. Klein disagreed and maintained that what Claire really wanted was the freedom to create clothes as she envisioned them and he believed that putting the McCardell name on the label would in fact only heighten her sense of loyalty to Townley. Adolph Klein was right.

Taking up their old showrooms at 550 Seventh Avenue, Klein and Geiss reassembled much of the original Townley crew. Claire's pattern maker, Bessie Susteric, who stayed with McCardell for more than twenty years, returned to the workrooms, as did Harry Friedman, Geiss's original production man. Friedman, a McCardell loyalist from the designer's very first years with Townley, remembered Claire as "the one who kept the workroom together."[5] In keeping with the designer's request, Townley's offices and showroom, which had been rather nondescript during McCardell's early days there, were redecorated to Claire's rather singular specifications— austere black walls in one area, navy in others, her favorite beige in another, bright white in the main foyer. As an added McCardell touch, a glossy black linoleum floor was laid down throughout. In addition to creating a dramatic effect, Townley's new look was in high contrast to the pastel-and-mirrored boudoir look found in the showrooms of many of Townley's competitors. More to the point, it provided a striking modern backdrop against which McCardell's line was shown to buyers and to the press.

McCardell, who was always at the center of the action in the sample room, preferred whenever possible to be absent during the recurring warfare over such hot topics as shoulder pads and the added expense of pockets. Geiss believed they were unnecessary, Claire insisted upon them in every garment. McCardell felt that beyond their obvious use for carrying things, pockets offered a lady "a place to put one's hands so as not to feel ill at ease or vulnerable." With Adolph Klein on board, gone were the days of Geiss's panicked responses to her more daring designs: the new arrangements made the workroom off-limits to Geiss, and rather surprisingly even to Klein, who promised that Claire's designs would be made up exactly as she conceived them, pockets and all, without the all-too-familiar "suggestions" she had grown to expect whenever Geiss and fashion buyers got into the same room.

The new regime, headed by Klein, placed McCardell at a great advantage, for she was finally free to create what she wanted. More important, even the clothes that were most "outlandish" (Geiss's word) were as much a part of her showings as were her "bread and butter" dresses (McCardell's words). Still, things were pulled from the collection if orders were low or if they were too expensive to produce, but not without McCardell's prior knowledge and consent. No longer would the more adventurous or problematic McCardells end up hidden on the sample rack in the back room while Geiss's reps showed only what they felt to be the most salable of McCardell's creations.

Autonomy of this kind was all but unheard of within the American garment industry of the 1940s. At the time, most mid-market American clothing manufacturers, if not copy houses slavishly geared to Parisian dictates, were deferential to the likes and dislikes of the store buyers. Throughout her career, Claire could look to Adolph Klein with loyal appreciation and gratitude for his unconventional blanket of protection much in the manner of a patron of the arts.

Joset Walker, with whom Claire had remained friends since their Parsons days, made clear just how rare McCardell's free rein behind the drafting board was: "I can't tell you how I envied Claire," Walker once told *Life* magazine's Sally Kirkland, and then went on to describe how after her own collections were shown to the press, her conservative, bottom-line employer David Goodstein would "whisk all the most exciting things off the racks and hide them in his office closet,"[6] because he feared the response of more traditional buyers.

Adolph Klein, as well as Henry Geiss, were remarkable in that they allowed McCardell to design more or less as she pleased. By granting Townley's designer the freedom to cross over into such diverse categories as evening wear, tennis skirts, day wear, play clothes, ski clothes, and bathing

Plaid silk playsuit, 1942. Photographed on location at the Rose Pauson House, a Frank Lloyd Wright residence in Arizona. McCardell's bloomer-legged bubblesuit was selected and styled for *Harper's Bazaar* by legendary fashion editor Diana Vreeland. The photographer, Louise Dahl-Wolfe, and McCardell became close friends. Photo, Louise Dahl-Wolfe. Center for Creative Photography, University of Arizona

Three-piece playsuit ensemble.
Cotton, cotton knit, 1946.
Fashion Institute of Technology.
Gift of Adrian McCardell.
72.61.59A–C

Wool jersey tube dresses from the mid-1940s. At a time when casual dressing was just coming into its own. McCardell stopped apologizing for sportswear and stepped forward with casual clothes that could be worn almost anywhere. Photo, Irving Penn, 1950. Courtesy *Vogue*

McCardell designed winter activewear and play clothes for
women like herself who were just as apt to take up skiing and
bicycling in the winter months as they were to swim and play
tennis in the summertime. Here, a cold weather cycling
ensemble: box-pleated woolen knee pants and wool jersey
pullover with Claire's signature Superman hood. Photo,
Kay Bell, 1944. Courtesy *Vogue*

suits, Geiss and Klein not only broadened their potential customer base, but
in the process discovered that American women were ready to buy considerably more than just the afternoon tea dresses and golf skirts Townley Frocks
had previously offered. At the wholesale level, the small, privately owned specialty shops found this unsurpassed design range especially appealing. In an
era when most designers and manufacturers were limited to narrow categories
such as coats and dresses, evening clothes, or sports clothes, McCardell and
the new Townley were selling raincoats and swimwear alongside floor-length
taffeta gowns and tweed suits. Buyers from smaller stores soon realized that
McCardell's widely diversified collections made it possible to buy for several
departments at once, and as a result they often bought more. During her first
three years back at Townley, while McCardell's reputation and following grew
steadily, Townley's business literally tripled. It didn't happen immediately,
however, and Klein once remarked that in the first few seasons the "only way
we stayed in business," was that buyers "started catching on to her old things
while they were laughing at her new ones," and pointed out that people had
never seen "anything like the things Claire dreamed up."[7]

Though Claire McCardell and Adolph Klein continued their close association for almost twenty years, when asked in later years how Townley's
designer came up with some of her more adventurous designs, Klein, who
was known to describe McCardell's work in terms ranging from "a guaranteed home run" to "some damned weird stuff," replied with his hands in
the air, "These women—you never know where they get their inspiration
from. It may be a crack in the wall."[8]

That fateful elevator ride of McCardell, Klein, Geiss, and Friedman
proved to be a one-way trip to the top for McCardell's career. By successfully
aligning mass production and high style together for the first time in the
history of fashion, Claire McCardell Clothes brought moderately priced,
well-designed American sportswear to an eagerly awaiting market. With
Townley's new structure allowing each to do what they did best, the team of
McCardell and Klein effectively helped to expand and redefine both the
style—and national identity—of modern American women.

In fact, before McCardell and a small circle of other American sports
and leisurewear designers, such as Tina Leser, Tom Brigance, and Carolyn
Schnurer, sportswear as we know it today seems to have happened by accident. Townley Frocks, for instance, in the 1930s described itself in press
releases as a moderate to better market line of women's apparel for "spectator sports and active leisure." Was the Townley customer an athlete or a
"lady" spectator? The ambiguity could be read in Townley's own logo and
dress tag: the image of a woman in golf clothes, with her club in mid-stroke.
The identity problem was more confusing in the array of garments Townley
showed to prospective store buyers, which included golfwear as well as
Paris-inspired eveningwear.

Whereas Townley and other manufacturers like it continued to promote
this two-dimensional portrait of the American woman (which the fashion

Citing the freedom afforded by the deep pockets and generously cut armholes in men's clothes, McCardell once commented, "Men are free of the clothes problem. Why shouldn't I follow their example?" Red slubbed wool suit with patch pockets, late 1940s.

press also endorsed), McCardell addressed all the rest of the hours of the day: real life, in other words, lived by real women. With her designs, McCardell seemed to be saying, Forget Paris. Forget Seventh Avenue. McCardell had stopped apologizing for sportswear and stepped forward with honest, well-designed wearable clothes. Speaking to reporters in the 1950s, McCardell modestly insisted that her success was due in part to "good timing" and in part to the fact that her designs focused on the women who wore them. McCardell felt that only another American, and more specifically a woman, could fully understand the needs of an American lifestyle.

Day dress and belt. Cotton, leather, c. 1949.
Fashion Institute of Technology. Gift of
Janet Chatfield Taylor, 69.154.6AB

Claire's fascination with menswear design
was to remain with her throughout her
career. From the late 1940s, a masterfully
mitered cotton shirtwaist dress with its
bias-cut bodice and McCardell's favorite
sleeve: cut on the bias and all in one with
the bodice. The paneled skirt is cut on
the straight grain and pieced horizontally,
creating an optical visual effect when seen
from the front.

World War II

By the time the United States joined the war in 1941, American industry had already begun to feel the sudden shortage of domestic manpower and turned to women, who began entering the workforce in unprecedented numbers. McCardell was aware of the social implication of this mobilization of the nation's female population and responded with low-cost dresses and separates cut from heavy denim, durable cottons, and comfortable wool jersey. With useful, deep pockets and no-frills styling, Claire's wartime outfits appealed equally to students, office and factory workers, and the overworked housewife. McCardell's designs addressed the needs of women like herself who were active (often in the workplace) and needed moderately priced clothes that were versatile, well made, and easy to care for. Her buttonless, roll-up sleeves and reinforced double top-stitched seams were as practical as they were appealing, and despite the war, reflected the designer's longstanding belief in sensible clothes.

In 1942, in an effort to conserve raw materials for the war effort, the U.S. Production Board issued fabric restrictions to the garment industry. In addition to limiting usage of particular fibers, guidelines, known as the L–85 order, specified the exact yardage of fabric that designers could use. While some designers may have found these restrictions daunting, McCardell seemed to have found them inspiring. With her early, even voluntary, use of inexpensive, utilitarian fabrics and natural tendency toward leaner, unfussy silhouettes, McCardell was perfectly attuned to the wartime sensibility. Having grown bored with the ubiquitous floral prints that fabric salesmen had been showing her, Claire was already accustomed to searching alternative markets for unlikely fabric possibilities. Mattress ticking, children's prints, even lingerie fabrics had already found their way into McCardell's collections; never did they give the impression of being stand-ins for other, less readily available fabrics. When the government declared a surplus on weather balloon cottons in 1944, McCardell ordered it by the truckload, and soon American women were wearing it with pride. The same with butcher's apron linen and rayon failles: McCardell simply refused to overlook a fabric's hidden potential, regardless of its accustomed use. After all, once the renegade fabrics had been cut into one of McCardell's sleek, feminine looks, who knew or cared that it had been earmarked for tablecloths at the local eatery? To the contrary, Americans applauded Claire's remarkable dexterity and creative contributions to fashion during the economic crunch caused by World War II. Her smartly mitred shirtwaist dresses, which sold yearly in the tens of thousands were, almost without exception, sewn from fabrics ordered by McCardell from mills in the South which normally supplied the men's dress shirt and pajama market. A brutal critic of poor quality, McCardell soon earned the respect of the mill owners whose remnants she had purchased early in her career; eventually she became an influential presence in the preseason ordering and pattern approval for more than one cotton mill.

Lauren Bacall, in her early years modeling McCardell's wartime denim coverall. Like McCardell, Bacall's look was more scrubbed clean than made up. McCardell's pared-down utilitarian wartime designs were both economical and sensible. Photo, Louise Dahl-Wolfe, 1943. Center for Creative Photography, University of Arizona

Afternoon dress. Cotton gauze, lace. c. 1945. Fashion Institute of Technology.
Gift of Vivian Cousins, 87.11.1
Again the appearance of the designer's signature spaghetti string ties.
Found on nearly everything from her Monastic dress to her bathing suits,
these immediately recognizable "McCardellisms" were literally several yards
long and could be tied in any number of ways.

One McCardell innovation that remained popular even after the war was Claire's wrap-and-tie designs that eliminated the need for increasingly scarce zippers and metal closures. The shortage of metals actually gave McCardell a chance to prove the efficiency of her self-tailoring waist-knotting blouses and pullover bias-cut jersey dresses—yards of semi-attached spaghetti string ties were stitched in place just under the bust with the length left free for the wearer to create for herself the most flattering waistline.

Gouache rendering by Claire McCardell
of the Kitchen Dinner dress, 1941.
Brooklyn Museum of Art. Special Collections

By this time, McCardell's fascination with closures of all kinds had become evident: self-ties handily accommodated wartime restrictions, and fasteners of all types came under Claire's close scrutiny. Disenchanted with the unreliability and variable quality of the first commercially available zippers, McCardell turned to eyelets, hooks, clips, and metal closures of all kinds when they could be acquired outside of the war restrictions. Born, no doubt, of her early fascination with French couture, this interest in small-scale, high-quality, hand-picked trimmings and fit-sensitive closures gave Claire's designs the feel of custommade dresses, or at least dresses costing many times more than hers did. One pet peeve of McCardell's, however, was the ubiquitous back zipper or any clothing that a woman needed help

getting in and out of. Insistent that "a woman may live alone and like it, but you may soon come to regret it if you wrench your arm trying to zip a back zipper into place." Claire almost always avoided back closures.[9] Even when zippers became available after the war, McCardell still shunned them, preferring buttons, sashes, or hooks instead—even on pants. When McCardell did use zippers, they were often visibly placed as a design accent.

Seeing that World War II had dramatically changed the way many women lived, McCardell accurately intuited that having worked outside the home, many of the newly employed American women would be reluctant to return exclusively to the role of housewife when the troops came back. McCardell's designs offered solutions for women who chose to walk either path, or who, Claire included, opted for both. In 1941, McCardell showed her first Kitchen Dinner dress, a cotton shirtwaist with a full, flowing feminine skirt complete with its own matching apron for women like herself who like to cook but don't want to look the part. The practical, spirited look of the Kitchen Dinner dress loosely resembled the traditional barmaid dresses from the Alsace-Lorraine region of France and the mountain villages of northern Germany. It became popular with housewives, including those who found themselves without domestic help for the first time.

To a large degree, it was during the war years that McCardell came into her own as a designer. With so much of American industry dedicated to war concerns, McCardell's simply cut and inexpensively produced designs were in harmony with the American wartime sensibilities. Additionally, Claire became known for appealing and innovative methods of stepping around wartime restrictions. One great triumph was Claire's solution to the severe rubber and leather restrictions that had promptly led to shoe rationing. While manufactured leather shoes were strictly rationed during the war, ballet slippers were not. In 1944, McCardell went ahead and made an appointment with Capezio, a company that supplied dancers and performers with toe shoes and warm-up slippers. She showed up with fabric swatches in her hand and within weeks Capezio had produced for Townley the unrestricted heel-less, lace-up, and slip-on ballerina styles in fabrics that matched or accented McCardell's current collection. When Claire's models appeared in the showrooms wearing the ballet slippers they were met with applause. Though originally intended for at-home use, McCardell's flat shoes promptly became a big hit and started a trend which was eventually adopted by upscale designers, including Valentina. McCardell had inadvertently launched a business in flat shoes for Capezio. For many years, McCardell would style shoes for the company and Capezio would produce whatever she wanted for her collections— even if it meant cheetah-skin ankle booties, or red-and-black striped nylon rain boots to match a raincoat.

During the war, many of America's chicest women prided themselves in showing their wartime respects by dressing in a restrained, even somber manner. By 1941, with the French couture industry at a standstill because

Wool jersey wedding dress with coif, 1941. As a result of an innate sense of how fabrics performed on the body, McCardell often arrived at the extraordinary by way of the unexpected. Photo, Don Honeyman, 1941. Courtesy *Vogue*

of the war, wartime fashions nevertheless remained more or less frozen within the lines of the broad-shouldered Schiaparelli silhouette. Wartime wardrobes consisted of tailored suits with nipped-in waists and narrow, below-the-knee skirts cut from sturdy worsted wools and coating fabrics. With broad shoulders as their only truly definitive characteristic, they became known as "victory suits" and left an indelible imprint on mid-century fashion. Due largely to the social implications and immediate spread of this utilitarian fashion during the war years, the "victory suit" obscured many of the more unusual and innovative wartime fashions.

By contrast, McCardell's designs of the early 1940s emphasized the importance of play clothes and the dress, instead of the suit, in an effort to counter the masculine feel of the wartime uniform. McCardell, who rarely designed clothing that would be described merely as "pretty," nevertheless refused to yield to the widespread belief that tasteful wartime fashions should avoid seeming *feminine*. Though austerity had become a psychological component of the patriotic mindset, by the end of the war the average American woman's wardrobe had acquired a masculine flavor which, McCardell contended, could stand a little kidding. Starting in the early 1940s Claire's collections suggested fashions not only by silhouette and color, but also by concept and feel, which the designer communicated by the names she gave to each dress and each new detail presented. Her surviving notebooks and desk notes are full of such lists, with collection dates and small sketches all on the same pages. Some of the more amusing examples which began merely as quickly jotted phrases and eventually found their way into America's closets include: "Hobo patches," "scarecrow silhouette," "bandanna necklines," "Superman hood," "saggy armholes," "turkey tail brown," "beet soup" red, and even a wartime skirt with multicolored patches called "Salvage Sally."[10]

As Claire's designs began to prove themselves in the marketplace and she came into her own at Townley, "Claire McCardell Clothes" came to represent more the designer's own ideas and less Townley's lingering conservatism. In particular, shoulder pads, a prewar and wartime staple, began with rare exception to disappear from the McCardell line. Claire had long promoted sensibly cut clothing that was loyal to the body first, and to fashion second, and believed that no condition existed under which overconstructed clothing was justifiable: "I like comfort in the rain, in the sun, for active sports, comfort for sitting still and looking pretty."[11] Nearly always without shoulder pads or designed to be worn without a bra, noticeably casual, and subtly sexy, the look of Claire McCardell Clothes during the 1940s was aptly summed up by one fashion editor as more Lauren Bacall than Betty Grable.

Cocktail dress. Silk faille. c. 1944. Fashion Institute of Technology. Gift of Adrian McCardell. 72.61.163 By emphasizing the importance of the dress instead of the suit, McCardell offered American women a more feminine alternative to the hard-lined silhouettes that were ubiquitous during World War II.

Pop-ova
1942

"Pop-Over"
Reg. U. S. Pat., Off.

THE ORIGINAL
UTILITY FASHION
DESIGNED BY
Claire McCardell

Household
device de-luxe for
busy women. Gay, practical pina-
fore that you can wear by itself or
over your dress. Equally at home in
the kitchen, at play or outdoors. So
becoming you can greet your guests in
it. Has capacious, quilted, catch-all
pocket. Quilted mitt swings from waist-
band. Striped and plain washable cottons. Sizes 10 to 20. $6 95
In New York at
LORD & TAYLOR
and at better stores everywhere, or write TOWNLEY FROCKS, 550 Seventh Avenue, N.Y.C

Dress Patented

Originally created in blue denim, the Pop-over
eventually became available in cotton gingham, silk,
corduroy, even winter-weight wools.

The Pop-over

During the war, *Harper's Bazaar* fashion editor Diana Vreeland and editor-in-chief Carmel Snow presented McCardell with a challenge: Claire was asked to create a dress for the busy housewives and mothers who, still with an eye for style, were "faced with the facts of life" and were taking on their own household duties for themselves. McCardell delivered the Pop-over, a simple, self-aproned, wrap-front denim dress, which even came with an attached oven mitt. Selling for just $6.95, the Pop-over eventually sold into the hundreds of thousands. Insistent that women deserved to look and feel attractive even as homemakers, McCardell made the Pop-over a permanent part of each collection. But after the copyright problem with the Monastic dress in 1938, McCardell and Klein took another precaution: on November 24, 1942, the Pop-over was patented for three and one-half

Opposite:
Gouache rendering by McCardell of her original 1942
Pop-over dress, which sold into the hundreds of thousands.
The Pop-over remained in McCardell's line in some form
or another over the next 16 years. Brooklyn Museum
of Art, Special Collections

McCardell's first leotard designs were dubbed "funny tights" by *Life* magazine, and though the all-in-one jersey knits garnered media attention for their forward-looking originality, they later proved too expensive to produce for the designer's mid-market clientele. Photo, Nina Leen for *Life* magazine, 13 September, 1943. Courtesy Time, Inc.

LIFE

LEOTARDS

SEPTEMBER 13, 1943 **10** CENTS
YEARLY SUBSCRIPTION **$4.50**

years. And to ensure that this time Townley did not miss out on the subsequent copying craze, for the next two years the designer shrewdly knocked herself off first by providing several variations on the Pop-over for retailers such as Best & Co. who sold it under other names. One year the Pop-over might show up as a fully cut solid-colored cotton cover-up, the next it might appear in the form of a more tapered silhouette in checked cotton gingham. Evolving and being constantly updated, the Pop-over became a wearable testimonial to the common-sense practicality of Claire McCardell's design message.

In 1942, McCardell was awarded a citation of honor for the Pop-over by the panel judges of the American Fashion Critics' Award, which acknowledged the design as "an outstanding interpretation of fashion trends under the restrictive influences of 1941."[12] As a result of the citation, Townley's press coverage dramatically increased, and by mid-1943 the appearance of Claire McCardell Clothes in magazine editorials and advertisements had grown. Norman Norell had won out over Claire for his contribution to American fashion that year, accepting the first of what was to become the most coveted award in the fashion industry, the Coty Award. On the eve of his own retrospective in 1972, Norell (with whom Claire had worked while at Hattie Carnegie) demonstrated the esteem McCardell's contemporaries felt for her when he told a writer that McCardell "should have had that first Coty Award for American fashion back in 1943 instead of me. Don't forget, Claire invented all of those marvelous things strictly within the limits of mass production. I worked in the couture tradition—expensive fabrics, hand stitching, exclusivity, all that—but Claire could take five dollars worth of common cotton calico and turn out a dress a smart woman could wear anywhere."[13]

With a flair for the unusual and a keen understanding of how fabrics worked on the body, McCardell had the confidence to raise familiar fabrics to the realm of the extraordinary, merely by way of the unexpected. One of Claire's most talked-about designs of the wartime period was her all-in-one wool jersey leotard and pullover sweater looks which even landed the designer the cover of *Life* magazine in 1943. Though McCardell had long promoted the benefits of wool jersey, the original idea for the leotards came from her longstanding friend and former schoolmate, Mildred Orrick, who had presented the leotard concept to *Harper's Bazaar* as a pitch for an editorial section.[14] Editors Carmel Snow and Diana Vreeland had liked Orrick's radical idea, but thought it might be better received if it were to come from a designer like McCardell, who at the time was quickly gaining a reputation for the unusual. Vreeland had firsthand experience with McCardell's deft handling of wool jersey from the days when McCardell was still working for Hattie Carnegie, and knew the defiantly innovative designer was up to the task.

It seems other people thought so too: in early 1944, the second American Fashion Critics' Award was presented to Claire McCardell for her contribution to American fashion during the previous year. With the extraordinary success of the Pop-over in 1942, record sales at Townley in 1943, and the Coty Award the following year, McCardell's career surged forward with such momentum that it seemed life on Seventh Avenue just couldn't have gotten any better for the all-American designer. After more than a decade, Claire McCardell was finally making her mark on American fashion with her own "good numbers."

Also by this time Claire was married to her longtime beau, Irving Drought Harris, and had gone to live with Harris and his two young children, John and Elizabeth. Life as Mrs. Irving Harris seems to have been the one side of Claire McCardell that occasionally contradicted her otherwise ragingly independent character. While Harris remained an avid socializer and was prone to attend charity benefits and hobnob with the

Ensemble: culottes and hooded top.
Wool knit. c. 1952. Fashion Institute of
Technology. Gift of Sally Kirkland.
76.33.7AB

The Superman hood of 1942 was originally
designed as part of McCardell's personal
ski ensembles. She later incorporated it into
her professional line, adapting it for everything
from beach coverups to wedding gowns.

moneyed leisure set on Fisher's Island where the couple had acquired a weekend cottage, the reclusive McCardell still preferred ski weekends with one or two friends, and often went on her own to the farmhouse in Frenchtown to get away from the New York social circuit. Perhaps most surprising was the decor of the couple's eleven-room Fifth Avenue apartment, which was decidedly not Claire's taste but markedly heavy in an English clubroom manner. The family joke ran that whereas at Townley she answered to no one, at home Claire submitted swatches to Harris for approval first.[15] A friend of McCardell's who visited the couple's home often said the only exception was Claire's own room, which had gay red painted walls, organdy curtains, English costume prints, and Japanese figures in shadow boxes adorning the walls.[16] A surprise to no one, the designer who became famous for her shirtwaist dresses also collected prints by Charles Dana Gibson.

Those who knew Claire personally readily recognized that it was the active, outdoorsy side of her life that supplied the inspiration for the McCardell fashion empire: the chilly gusts of wind that led her to draw her turtleneck sweaters up around her ears while racing down the ski slopes ultimately brought about the hooded Superman knit tops which became immensely popular by the early 1940s. Claire always designed clothing that served a purpose and was born of necessity, clothes that spoke clearly of the designer's attention to solving problems. In keeping with her belief that a woman's choice of clothes should be determined more by her way of life than by anything else, McCardell's most consistent source of inspiration for her collections was throughout her life to remain herself and the life she led.

In 1943, Claire married Irving Drought Harris, an architect from Texas. Reclusive by nature, McCardell shunned Harris's ambitious New York social life whenever possible, preferring instead to spend time alone or with a small circle of close friends at the farmhouse she and Harris owned in Frenchtown, New Jersey.

The American Look

One of the first buyers Adolph Klein had called upon in 1940

Opposite:
Hostess dress and sash. Wool, 1955.
Fashion Institute of Technology.
Gift of Sally Kirkland, 76.33.11AB

As a champion of wool jersey,
McCardell had been wearing her
multipiece jersey separates since 1931.
It took more than 10 years before buyers
and magazine editors came to recognize
the practicality and inherent modernity
of this forward-looking system of dressing.
Photo, Kay Bell, 1946. Courtesy *Vogue*

Cocoa brown cotton off-the-shoulder wrap-front
dress, 1946
At a time when cotton had not yet earned its place
among designer fabrics, McCardell surprised textile
suppliers when she demanded that they not show her
"anything that couldn't be washed!" Courtesy *Vogue*

when McCardell had barely finished her

first samples for the new Townley was Marjorie Griswold. Griswold was a
buyer for Lord & Taylor, at the time one of America's most progressive
retailers of European and American fashion. Klein had asked Griswold for
an appointment to show her "something new and exciting." "Of course, they
all said that," Griswold later remarked, but she went over to the showroom
anyway and remembered that she "really sat up when the first dress came
out." [1] That first dress, in all its McCardell simplicity, caused Griswold to
place an order for Lord & Taylor before she had left Klein's office, and began
what would prove be the most influential relationship of Claire McCardell's
entire career. In an interview with then-journalist Betty Friedan some sev-
enteen years later, Griswold said, "I came to be nice," and remembered
thinking that before McCardell, "sports clothes were all the same anyhow,
straight and square—so dull. And then I saw this simple collarless dress,
dark stitched in white like blue jeans. I stopped being a good Samaritan.
This was original." [2]

Suit (front and rear views). Wool. 1946.
Fashion Institute of Technology.
Gift of Hood College. 96.61.12AB
Well-versed in couture sewing techniques.
McCardell's constructions nevertheless
maintained a boldness and wit that were
distinctly American. Here, fine tailoring
techniques and a sense of visual proportion
enhance the striped pattern of the wool suit.

Designs such as this cotton windowpane two-piece halter dress of 1946 earned McCardell a reputation as a designer for the very young. Photo, John Rawlings, 1953. Courtesy *Vogue*

At Lord & Taylor, under the shrewd and watchful eye of Dorothy Shaver, the company's first female president (and an important figure in the history of fashion retailing), Marjorie Griswold was fast gaining a reputation for bringing new designers to the attention of an American public, that she accurately intuited was ready for a fresh departure from the Eurocentric styles being offered by the majority of Seventh Avenue wholesalers. After a decade-long career of working her way up through the ranks at Macy's and a two-year hiatus from New York to try her hand at domestic life, Griswold had returned to fashion because of a tempting offer from Lord & Taylor and the opportunity to collaborate with Dorothy Shaver, who was making the kind of fashion waves for which Griswold already had a reputation.

Marjorie Griswold's experience was accordingly rewarded at Lord & Taylor with considerable liberty in the selection and showcasing of those designers whom she felt had the greatest talent and commercial potential for the store. Responsible for the introduction and initial retail support of such fashion innovators as Rudi Gernreich and Emilio Pucci, Griswold and Shaver also played key roles in orchestrating Claire McCardell's widespread public exposure.

For Claire McCardell, being taken under the wing of Marjorie Griswold was a major breakthrough. Over the first several years of their association, Griswold was quick to identify and appreciate many of McCardell's least understood design concepts, and she often gave Claire a chance to try out some of her more radical ideas in the marketplace when other buyers had shied away. Since 1934, McCardell had been trying to convince buyers that her five- and six-piece wool jersey separates system, which were hand washable and could be rolled up and tucked into a suitcase, offered the perfect solutions for the office, PTA, or 21 Club—day and evening alike. In Marjorie Griswold, McCardell not only found a buyer who understood her design concepts but also a progressive merchandiser who could bring them to the attention of the public just as fast as Adolph Klein could show them to her.

While other buyers had feared that McCardell's mix-and-match system of separates dressing was too sophisticated for their clientele, Griswold was confident that it was probably the buyers—and not American women—who actually required an explanation of this conceptually forward system of dressing. Fashion editor Sally Kirkland agreed, and pointed out that though, in hindsight, McCardell had been right on the mark with her pared-down, packable separates, she was going to have "to wait for merchandising to catch up."[3] Luckily for Claire McCardell, it seemed that with Marjorie Griswold and Dorothy Shaver on board, it was about to. Acceptance by the general public was going to take a little longer. In September of 1944, *Harper's Bazaar* ran an illustrated feature of McCardell's six-piece separates system. The group, which included a suit, a long skirt, pants, a bareback halter, and a knotted front blouse, was shown with the copy "Be nifty . . . Be new . . . Be interchangeable." New to some, perhaps, but the article hit the stands more than ten years after McCardell had first designed and begun showing the coordinated system to buyers. They may have taken a decade to catch on, but Claire herself had been wearing them all along.

Lord & Taylor's bold commitment to McCardell's forward-looking designs was not, however, without its ups and downs: Griswold remembered that many of McCardell's unconstructed wrap-and-tie designs lacked what in retailer's terms is referred to as "hanger appeal." With their yards of sashes or spaghetti string ties, many McCardells really only came to life (or "performed," as Claire would put it) when they were worn. As a result, many of the first McCardells that Lord & Taylor had purchased started at full price but often found their way to the markdown rack. Aware that it took a fairly sophisticated customer to understand McCardell's more "interactive" designs, Shaver and Griswold stood by their new designer and aggressively continued to promote McCardell's new take on American sportswear, despite slow sales in the first few seasons. Even in Claire's earliest designs for Lord & Taylor, Marjorie Griswold had caught glimpses of the look and clothes she felt American women wanted, but didn't yet know where to find, and eventually sold Shaver on the idea of promoting McCardell as a name designer in the main floor salon of Lord & Taylor's Fifth Avenue flagship store.

As Griswold's protégé designers began to build momentum in the marketplace, Lord & Taylor put into motion the advertising campaign that would promote their collections as "The American Look." Launched as a fully blown campaign in 1945, Lord & Taylor's "The American Look" program included nationally syndicated newspaper and magazine advertisements which quickly bolstered both the urban and grass-roots following of McCardell's distinctively American style, effectively linking the image of McCardell's designs with the designer's name and label. These hand-rendered full-page advertisements were drawn in a free-style manner, and were regularly placed in Sunday papers all across America. In a very short time, Claire McCardell was on her way to becoming a household word. From the early 1940s until the mid-1950s, McCardell enjoyed a major share of Lord & Taylor's advertising features and Townley eventually became the store's single largest domestic account.[4]

Though many published sources credit Lord & Taylor with having coined the term "The American Look," it actually had a predecessor. In the late 1920s, Best & Co., the same firm that had launched McCardell's Monastic dress to unprecedented sellout, had first used the term "The American Look" in conjunction with advertising copy and in-house merchandising under the direction of Mary Lewis, who for many years was Best's advertising director.[5] Involved in the styling and design of much of Best & Co.'s early fashion and accessories, Lewis was still, at the time McCardell was on the rise, actively contributing to the design, marketing, and retailing of American fashion. In addition to opening her own shop, at one point in her career Lewis designed and coordinated the fashion departments and catalogue sales of Sears, Roebuck, Incorporated, one of America's largest retailers. Whether or not Lewis was personally known to McCardell,

During the 1940s and 1950s, Lord & Taylor heavily promoted the work of American designers. McCardell's name came to be associated with "The American Look," in part due to the designer's popularity.

the name "The American Look" had already been in circulation before; Lord & Taylor simply had the good marketing sense to reintroduce it, featuring McCardell's clothes.

In addition to Claire McCardell, Lord & Taylor's "The American Look" program promoted other sportswear designers such as Tina Leser, Clare Potter, Carolyn Schnurer, Tom Brigance, and Bonnie Cashin who, like McCardell, were popular with the collegiate set and were enlightened to a more casual, American lifestyle-oriented mode of dressing. But McCardell's overwhelming commercial success in the years following her first appearance at Lord & Taylor gradually began to throw her competitors in the shade, and soon "The American Look" came to be associated with the ease and elegance of "Claire McCardell Clothes." Whether featuring a McCardell design or not, the fashions promoted in "The American Look" program at Lord & Taylor offered American women and retailers a proud alternative to imported or Paris-inspired styles that really did not always suit the needs of their thoroughly American lives.

In the early 1940s, perhaps by instinct or perhaps by necessity, Shaver and Griswold moved to promote American fashion at precisely the moment Paris was under siege by the Germans. Temporarily freed from the tyranny of Paris couture, a window of opportunity had opened for American designers. Though Paris would ultimately maintain its position as an international fashion and cultural center, Shaver and Griswold felt that with media support, American designers could step forward and prove that they were up to the task of dressing the nation.

Being cut off from France had no measurable effect whatsoever on Claire McCardell, who, perhaps more than any other American designer, would remain consistently unmoved by the whims of Paris couture. In fact, since 1940, she had graciously declined to visit the couture shows whenever in Paris, explaining that she did not wish to be influenced by the fanfare and spectacle of the events. "I for one am strongly influenced by what I see," McCardell told a reporter almost fifteen years after her last couture show, "and I am afraid if I went to the collections I might start making French clothes!"[6] McCardell had learned the French methods of construction and respected their standards of quality, but was insistent throughout her lifetime that America needn't look to foreign shores to meet the clothing needs of the modern American woman. What Claire McCardell reasoned, and quite rightly, was that what may very well be perfect for a duchess didn't always suit the American Mrs. Jones.

McCardell's emergence as the precursor of "The American Look" was the predictable result of the long-running ad campaigns and in-house promotions at Lord & Taylor. As a result, McCardell is often spoken of as being "the creator of The American Look," and then, by association, "the creator of American sportswear." But perhaps Claire McCardell would be more accurately remembered as casual attire's most ardent and influential proponent. Though American sportswear unquestionably owes much to this innovative and independent American designer, McCardell herself often pointed out that she was one among an admittedly small but passionately dedicated coterie of youthful leisure and sportswear designers who believed in dressing American women in keeping with the way American women actually lived. In truth, American sportswear actually created itself, in an ongoing social evolution dating from the nineteenth century. Much as McCardell's designs reflected changes in American women's lives, in keeping with her natural modesty, at no point in her lifetime did the designer from Maryland ever claim to be the sole source of the trend toward casual dressing.

Despite this fact, today McCardell is generally remembered more often in terms of her "legend" and less in terms of her specific and truly remarkable contributions to American fashion. In McCardell's case, however, the legend was not self-induced. It grew out of esteem for Claire McCardell's original talent, her refusal to bow to Parisian fashion dictates, and her canny ability to celebrate a casual, relaxed, and wholly American lifestyle. McCardell had become a symbol of American success. Aside from being

Many of McCardell's more unusual designs were met with enthusiasm by magazine editors and the press. This knit tube pullover wrap from 1947 was unlike anything buyers had seen and soon it was featured in *Harper's Bazaar*. With this kind of publicity, the sweater sold out immediately in its first season. Photo. Louise Dahl-Wolfe. 1947. Center for Creative Photography. University of Arizona

Halter top and skirt.
Cotton pique, 1950s.
Fashion Institute of Technology.
Gift of Adrian McCardell, 72.61.91AB
In an attempt to put new life into
an old dress, McCardell once drew
up the ends of an evening dress
and secured them with a safety pin.
Hence the inspiration for the skirt
of this elegant two-piece halter dress.

THE NEWS:
EARLY JERSEY

THE NEWS:
TAUPE MINK

Left: A completely new mink mutation called "Aleutian." A subtle taupe that purrs in a minor key and has, under its glistening guard hairs, hints of blue and grey. The finger-tip jacket (probably the most useful fur shape going) is a triumph of softness, with a murmur of collar, slight shoulders. A Ritter design of EMBA "Aleutian" mink. Harzfeld's; Famous-Barr. Suède hat; Mr. John. Ceylon sapphire and diamond earrings; Van Cleef & Arpels. Glentex silk scarf, at Best's. Compliment to taupe, Barbara Gould's "Coral Flame" lipstick.
Right: A grey worsted jersey dress, its width pleated, shaped and corded to a flat-falling narrowness. By Claire McCardell, $45; from Lord & Taylor; Garfinckel's; Neiman-Marcus. Tall, thin umbrella handle; from Uncle Sam Umbrella Shop. Head-clutching grey flannel hat, from John Frederics.

HORST

Coco Chanel with Serge Lifar, c. 1930. Like Chanel, McCardell helped popularize casual attire. Both women eschewed corseted styles and padding in favor of soft wool jerseys with their inherent elegance.

Opposite:
Monastic pleated wool jersey dress, 1949. McCardell's insistence that well-designed fashions "somehow earn the right to survive" led her to reproduce successful designs from past seasons with slight variations. The Monastic first appeared in 1938 and remained part of McCardell's collections throughout her career. Photo, Horst. Courtesy *Vogue*

a brilliant promotional tool for Lord & Taylor, "The American Look" served to heighten the acceptance of and pride in American-made goods. As if describing "The American Look," McCardell once characterized the inspiration she drew from the life and pace of American women by saying, "For me it is American—what looks and feels like America. It's freedom, it's democracy, it's casualness, it's good health. Clothes can say all that." [7]

Beyond their respective mythologies, Claire McCardell was essentially doing for America what Coco Chanel had done before her in France— designing and popularizing a way of dressing that made casual elegance not only acceptable but desirable—although at completely opposite ends of the market. Similarities to Chanel do not end there, however, and though few fashion buyers would ever use Chanel's and McCardell's names in the same sentence, the two style makers, each from distinctively different social vantage points and with almost mutually exclusive clientele, were often thinking along similar lines. If McCardell can be said to have designed with a nod to Vionnet and Madame Grès, upon close examination she seems in certain

Swimwear group, left to right: Bathing suit. Wool jersey, 1950. Gift of Carol Mann, 72.81.1; Diaper bathing suit. Wool jersey, 1970s copy of 1942 original. Gift of Laura Sinderbrand, 72.116.1; Bathing suit. Wool jersey, metal hooks, c. 1953. Gift of John McCardell, 87.144.9. All, Fashion Institute of Technology

instances to have thought an awful lot like Coco Chanel. Beyond their
superficial similarities (both were fond of sports, wearing men's clothes,
deep pockets in nearly all of their clothes, and a playful excess of costume
jewelry) there are remarkable parallels in their seemingly disparate ap-
proaches to dressing women. In particular, both McCardell and Chanel
made extensive and noticeable use of signature hardware in the design
and construction of their clothing (McCardell's brass hooks, eyes, and clips;
Chanel's lead weights, stitched-in hem chains, and cast buttons). Both
women, even during their lifetimes, were charged with being "rebellious"
and were equally reactionary against existing fashion norms, unequivocally
dismissing uncomfortable, corseted, and uplifted fashion as mere bad habit.
Promoting the flexibility and comfort of knit fabrics, both McCardell and
Chanel were champions of wool jersey, and from opposite sides of the
Atlantic both women waged their own private wars against structured,
form-altering clothing and remained wary of male couturiers' ability to
conceive of or create comfort in women's clothes.

Like Chanel, McCardell was prone to developing and maintaining identifiable classics (Chanel's suits and grosgrain seam bindings, McCardell's

Pop-over and Monastic styles, sashes and string ties) which remained part of their collections for decades—updated but never drastically changed. Claire McCardell, however, here quite unlike Coco Chanel, had seemingly little interest in being credited with being "first," offering instead that her own clothes were the direct result of infusions of inspiration into situations where, as she once put it, "more appropriate and appealing clothing for women could be created."[8] Demonstrating none of the feigned modesty of many successful couturières, the shy, almost reclusive McCardell was more concerned with the performance of her designs when worn by women than by their inscrutable originality in the eyes of the press. When interviewed about her clothes, McCardell often referred to the process of designing clothes as "solving problems"—a successful garment supported her demands of functionality and performance.

Seeing that McCardell had proven herself capable of designing for nearly any category straight across the board, Adolph Klein had more than once proposed to Claire that they consider the children's clothing market. After having sidestepped this for many seasons, McCardell finally gave in

Diaper suit in black wool jersey. Photo. John Rawlings. 1944. Courtesy *Vogue*

Playsuit with belt. Cotton, elastic, brass, 1954. Fashion
Institute of Technology. Gift of Sally Kirkland. 76.33.40
Like her swimsuits, McCardell's playsuits were anything
but conventional. The designer had long ago made
a decision not to follow the status quo, which was evident
in everything she designed.

In the late 1940s, Townley introduced a line of
children's clothing marketed as "Baby McCardells."
Photo, Christa Zinner, 1957

Opposite:
Black jersey bathing suit with pleated linen plaid skirt.
Photo, Genevieve Naylor, 1946

when Klein commented that with so many of her dresses already being
copied in the children's market, perhaps she was right not to bother adding more McCardells to the pot. That was all it took. For several years in
the late 1940s into the early 1950s, "Baby McCardells" were offered by
a host of major American department stores. In this market, however,
McCardell was going to encounter her first commercial glitch: the very
same construction techniques that she had so cleverly wielded to create
her cost-effective women's clothing cost just as much on a small garment;
consequently this pushed the price of Baby McCardells to the high end of
the children's market, making them more expensive than buyers expected
and therefore somewhat less "McCardell."

This was not the case, however, in the juniors market: the "Junior
Editions by Claire McCardell" label was a scaled-down collection based
largely on her regular lines with slightly less risqué necklines and more

youthful styling and colors. This limited production line was produced sporadically until the mid-1950s, and was intended for the prep school and urban teen set. Junior Editions were full of Claire's favorite touches: signature hardware, sashes, and even her sophisticated wool jersey. Yet they managed to remain more competitively priced within the juniors market than McCardell's baby clothes had been in theirs.

Updating her best sellers and most popular silhouettes, McCardell was not only quick to identify her own classics but went one step further in establishing what she called her "McCardellisms": those most readily identifiable McCardell details such as her signature metal fastenings, double rows of top-stitching, wrap-and-tie separates, spaghetti string ties and yard-long sashes.

In addition to designing her collections, McCardell also became actively involved in the marketing of her clothes, where she displayed a keen business sense. By the early 1940s, McCardell told Adolph Klein and Townley that to firmly establish both the label and the look of "Claire McCardell Clothes" it was necessary to continue producing and advertising best-selling styles from past collections—even designs from three or four years running. This very unlikely marketing approach was one of the very few business tips Klein ever took from McCardell, who rarely offered this kind of advice.

In hindsight, this approach to reissuing old designs and establishing a reputation for "timeless" clothes was a radical departure from the psychology that most designers and fashion editors exploited to their commercial advantage—the American woman's horror of being caught in last season's clothes. But advertising the past season's dresses? It almost seemed like an anti-fashion move. Not surprisingly for McCardell it produced the desired effect. In an uncharacteristically self-confident interview in 1951, McCardell proudly told a reporter, "You can take a dress of mine that you bought ten years ago, lower the hem, make a few accessory changes and wear it today—and it will still look good." [9] And indeed one could, for often it was the exact same dress. Consequently, a McCardell customer never felt from one season to the next that her last year's purchase was obsolete or would soon appear dated. It came to be accepted that a McCardell dress was no stranger to the coming season, any more than it had been to the last. The designer who had worn her rejected wool jersey separates for a decade before stores would sell them once made the sage observation that well-designed "fashions somehow earn their right to survive." [10] This philosophy, in addition to inspiring a loyal following among the nation's dress-buying public, assured even longtime customers that though McCardell's collections were always full of fresh, new ideas, there was somehow always something familiar to be found.

Occasionally, however, even Claire's most loyal customers temporarily deserted her. Though she had been selling backless dresses and braless halters to women across the nation for nearly a decade, her first swimwear designs of 1936 were considered too racy, even among the most sophisticated fashion buyers. To her credit, where McCardell was unconventional and posed a challenge to the established fashions of her day, she was rarely

Even on her swimwear, McCardell employed her signature brass hook-and-eye closures. Designs such as these often went from the beach to the lunch table with the addition of the designer's wraparound skirts (see page 93). Photo, John Rawlings, 1941. Courtesy *Vogue*

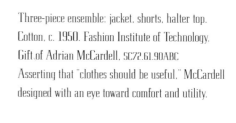

Three-piece ensemble: jacket, shorts, halter top.
Cotton, c. 1950. Fashion Institute of Technology.
Gift of Adrian McCardell. SC72.61.90ABC
Asserting that "clothes should be useful," McCardell
designed with an eye toward comfort and utility.

Ensemble, consisting of rain cape, jacket, skirt.
Cotton poplin, wool (cotton side of reversible cape is visible),
1947. Fashion Institute of Technology. Gift of Adrian
McCardell. 72.61.158ABC
Functionality and utility were always important to McCardell.
This streamlined reversible wool-lined cotton poplin rain cape
was more in keeping with the form-follows-function aesthetic
of the industrial design movement of the 1940s than it was
with the overtly decorative tone of mid-century fashion.

wrong, even if time was not always on her side. Though they took almost five years to reach the stores, her almost bare, unlined wrap-and-tie bathing suits from the late 1930s provide a perfect example of the designer's singular approach to fashion. These second-skin lightweight jersey creations were at striking odds with heavy, flounce swimwear offered on the market at the time. To Claire McCardell, and to the young women who wore and understood her clothes, her quick-dry suits (which came in their own drawstring jersey bag) were modern, both in their design and practicality. By the 1940s, they had evolved into the better known wool jersey versions, which Claire called the Diaper suit. Within a few seasons McCardell's body-skimming swimwear was being talked about and seen everywhere.

Defending her daring pared-down designs against the padded, matronly swimwear generally available, the designer insisted that a swimsuit by its very name "informs one of its intended purpose!" If it had seemed humorous to McCardell that a sizable group of American women wished to be dressed like Parisian demoiselles, it was inconceivable to her that there might be another group who proposed swimming in what she called "skater's dresses." In one of her rare imperious moments, McCardell countered buyers' concern that her unlined, unpadded suits were too sexy to be salable by saying that not only did she not understand all the fuss, but that she was "afraid that little girl dresses worn as bathing suits suggests regression." In another discussion on the topic, she added coolly, "Swimsuits are for swimming. If it's a dress you want, I have that, too." [11]

Despite the fuss, McCardell's next-to-nothing swimwear creations of 1943 were given such an enormous amount of media attention and corresponding amount of editorial coverage that in the end to everyone's surprise but her own, they were back ordered three seasons running, despite their relatively high prices.

The 1943 version of McCardell's Diaper bathing suit, a highly recognizable, even iconic McCardell design, became an immediate favorite of several American fashion photographers. *Vogue*'s John Rawlings and *Harper's Bazaar*'s Louise Dahl-Wolfe photographed it more than once for editorial features and for their own archives. With its Japanese origami-like elegance, the Diaper bathing suit earned its name as a result of its ingeniously simple one-piece construction: it tied around the neck and passed between the legs before being brought up around the waist, to suit the countour of the body. This virtuoso feat of all-in-one construction, which demonstrated a noticeable aversion to cutting into the fabric whenever possible, stemmed in part from a desire to minimize production costs, and it also reflected McCardell's intimate understanding of the principles and applications of her first fashion mentor, Madeleine Vionnet. Where the suit was imperceptibly seamed, it was to join the bias-cut top to the invisible waistline.

Uncomplicated, virtually carefree, and fitting in the palm of the hand, the "indecently bare" swimsuits that McCardell was called to defend as appropriate for swimming eventually made their way from the beach to the lunch table where more than a few sophisticated women wore them with linen skirts and a bevy of costume jewelry. A swimmer herself, McCardell had worn a version of the Diaper suit for years before it had gone into the production line up at Townley. In fact, Claire McCardell did more than go to lunch in her swimsuit. In several of McCardell's date books and on the margins of various programs and invitations, Claire sometimes jotted down what ensembles she planned to wear. Consider "diaper suit—black, taffeta skirt—big bracelets . . ." for a benefit dinner with the uptown crowd. Or "grey jersey anything, new red buckle belt, funny hat" for a ladies' luncheon in 1952. Throughout her career, McCardell's approach to fashion continuously ignored or even poked fun at both conventional expectations and what the designer felt were unnecessarily stagnant categories of dress.

Nearly forty years after her death, McCardell has maintained her reputation among the fashion and academic cartel as "the designer's designer." Designing clothing with an awareness of available manufacturing, McCardell, much like America's industrial design mavericks Raymond Loewy and Donald Deskey, looked to function and utility while addressing the dictates of mass production and American industry. The streamlined, often futuristic aesthetic inherent in the form-follows-function movement of the late 1930s and early 1940s had effectively seeped into most fields of progressive design. In 1943, reflecting McCardell's awareness of this change, the designer entertained the idea of once again changing the Townley label, this time to "Claire McCardell Clothes Construction." Prone to asserting authoritatively that "clothes should be useful," McCardell's design principles, even her own wardrobe, made no excuses for clothes that merely looked pretty: they had to earn their keep. Understandably, McCardell is remembered for her unerring vision of women's fashion free from unnecessary clutter or faddish decoration. "Clothes," as she preferred to call them, were meant to suit a purpose, the woman, the body.

McCardell's faith in the unrealized potential of American mass-production manufacturing and its ability to bring to the general public a standard of taste and quality that it had hitherto yet to accomplish, once led the designer to make a statement that nearly bordered on socialism: "I belong to a mass-production country where any of us, all of us, deserve the right to good fashion and where fashion must be made available to all." Claire's faith in American industry was her refusal to accept what many believed: that the move away from handmade clothes was a move away from quality. McCardell never thought the two were mutually exclusive, and she embraced technology and production advancements with the confidence of a craftsman familiar with his tools. Beyond this, McCardell's confident vision of American women fit well with the more positive and relaxed postwar American mindset. With the end of the war and the return of readily available goods and services on the horizon, McCardell's clothes offered the pride of an American-made product, while the name "The American Look" suggested a pronounced identity many Americans now felt. Elegant, easy, and relaxed, McCardell's

designs were free of the self-conscious chic of French design. Whether dressing Rosie the Riveter in workaday denim, or the Junior League college set, McCardell's wartime designs never had so much as a tinge of "make do" about them. Naturally, those women who first found out about Claire's clothes through her clever and highly publicized wartime innovations were destined to join the ranks of McCardell enthusiasts at the war's end.

With sportswear now moving even further from its early definition of golf skirts and riding habits, and casual dressing firmly in place as a permanent component of the American woman's wardrobe, McCardell's customer base broadened as even the more upscale, urban set came to recognize and gravitate toward the easy-to-wear day-to-day styles she had been promoting for nearly two decades. Gone were the days of Adolph Klein's compulsory explanations to buyers that Claire's more unconventional looks would soon be coming into their own; during the war years Claire McCardell had proven herself. In a sense, the war had helped the designer reach her customers: the common-sense practicality and down-to-earth styling she had promoted from the very beginning fit right into the no-frills sensibility of the war effort. Even to the café society set, McCardell offered a viable alternative to Paris—here was an American designer who understood the construction and fit of the French school, but who designed and made clothes for the active lifestyles of women with their feet firmly planted on American soil.

Following World War II, many fashion critics predicted a resurgence of the lavish and glamorous looks of the Parisian prewar styles. As testimony to the strength of her design principles, McCardell's clothes never wavered in their functionality and comfortable simplicity, either at the height of wartime restrictions or upon the return of plenty when these restrictions were lifted. Engaged in her own conscientious war against excessive decoration, McCardell's approach to design was likely to remain unaffected by either feast or famine in the marketplace. After proving to a nation during the war that sensible, well-cut clothing needn't be prohibitively expensive and that women needn't sacrifice comfort to fashion, why would she abandon the principles she had fought so hard to demonstrate to be of lasting utility?

Something very different was happening in Paris, however. In February of 1947, Dior's "New Look" was revealed to the world: narrow, softly rounded shoulders, fuller, more feminine skirts (with scads of fabric), and longer lengths. With her anti-1940s silhouettes, McCardell's waist-conscious, slim-shouldered looks and full, feminine skirts had inadvertently foreshadowed Dior's New Look. Though the two designers were working in radically different markets, both were sensitive to women's desire for unmistakably feminine, impeccably cut clothing—McCardell's less exaggerated look accommodated the wearer's comfort to the designer's silhouette.

In February of 1945, two years before Dior had presented the New Look, McCardell wrote an article for the *Washington Star* titled "Wardrobe Futures." In it, the progressive American designer encouraged the

Left:
Dress and sash. Silk shantung. c. 1945. Fashion Institute of Technology. Gift of Adrian McCardell. 76.61.104

Below:
Hostess dress. Cotton. 1947. Gift of Eve Auchincloss. 85.180.1; Chemise dress. Jersey. c. 1950s. Gift of Sally Kirkland. 76.33.17. Both. Fashion Institute of Technology Moderately priced between $40 and $60. McCardell's comfortable Empire-style dresses were easily afforded by young career women, and they looked sharp enough to wear out in the evening

Maurice Goldberg

development of high-tech performance fabrics such as stain-proof and elasticized stretch cottons, and went on to predict just how the silhouette of the future would take shape. At the height of the hard-shouldered silhouette of the mid-1940s, McCardell confidently derailed current fashion with the following prophetic vision: "Skirts are going to be longer and fuller, and shoulders are going to get rounder . . . After you've been in the fashion game long enough you can see a trend looming long before it is launched. . . . I showed round shoulders five years ago. . . . As for full skirts, mine have been as full as could be from the beginning." [12]

The profound weight of these pre-Dior predictions have never really been credited to Claire McCardell. McCardell's scope on dressing in the future extended far beyond American shores. In the same article McCardell went on to say, "One thing we can be sure about is that the wardrobe of the future will be global. . . . For many years to come we'll all be plane-minded, hence globe-minded, hence capsule-minded: The fewest number of costumes with the greatest number of possibilities. . . ." [13] Though she was supposedly speaking of fashions to come, the descriptions she gave sounded a lot like the clothes she had been making for almost two decades.

Accustomed to being at odds with current trends, and at a time when animal skins were not regularly found in most designers' repertoires, in the same article Claire made the accurate prediction that in years to come ". . . good leather is going to be acceptable to most designers." Not surprisingly, McCardell had a varied collection of thick, studded leather cuffs and bracelets, even ankle straps, which she had made for herself at the shoemaker's shop; she may have been the first American sportswear designer to show leather pants and skirts before the 1950s. Fake fur, another of Claire's idiosyncrasies, was an unexplored resource she felt certain was destined to become an immensely popular fad. Teased by Adolph Klein about her "fright furs" and her capricious "teddy bear" coats of the early 1950s, they were all but forgotten by up-market designers until the early 1980s when faux fur became a staple in fashionable young women's closets. At a time when chic women wore mostly sable, mink, or chinchilla, McCardell, who could have owned any fur she wanted (and had many), favored a host of odd stand-ins such as nutria, reindeer, squirrel, and sheared rabbit. Unlike the more conservative styles offered by the majority of furriers, McCardell had her own ideas made up in fun, even frivolous styles that were nonetheless warm and functional. Perhaps a perfect expression of the seemingly contradictory genius inherent in Claire McCardell's approach to fashion might be the waist-length cheetah jacket with outsized industrial metal clips which the designer wore on windy ski slopes.

Far surpassing her legendary reputation for being the creator of Lord & Taylor's "American Look" during the 1930s and 1940s, McCardell was creating a look that American women would continue to wear, and consistently return to, for the next half century.

McCardell embodied a dynamic combination of hard-edged modernism and the feminine ideals of her generation. Fond of fabrics that were soft to the touch, she nevertheless maintained a well-stocked arsenal of studded calfskin leather cuffs, collars, and anklets, all her own designs. Photo. Maurice Goldberg. c. 1940

McCardell
and
the
Media

Emerging as a powerful design voice of the 1940s, McCardell's representation

in the press built an impressive momentum in the wake of America's post-war restructuring. Despite continued French influence over American fashion, McCardell remained adamant that America was, and should remain, a fashion entity in its own right. One major factor contributing to McCardell's sustained media presence was the growing number of young fashion editors and stylists of the 1940s who had become some of her most devoted and satisfied customers: women working behind the scenes in the fashion industry appreciated McCardell's clothes as well as the fact that she designed with women like themselves in mind. Building on the popularity she had gained during the war years, McCardell continued to maintain the interest of the American press and buying public. She had become, in effect, the unofficial ambassador of "The American Look."

Early on, *Harper's Bazaar* editors Carmel Snow and Diana Vreeland had recognized that Claire McCardell would be a major player in the formation of twentieth-century American fashion. Her pioneering ideas about interchangeability, travel-conscious clothes, timeless styling, and multi-seasonal fabrications were revolutionary. By virtue of their diversity, McCardell's collections offered image makers of the period a rare flexibility in either dressing up the high-styled elegance inherent in her work, or choosing a more utilitarian angle, stressing the wearability and common-sense appeal of "Claire McCardell Clothes." With her offbeat philosophies on fashion, coupled with the versatility of her designs, McCardell offered an editorial angle suitable for just about any magazine's target market. This

Above:
In 1955, McCardell became the third fashion designer to be featured on the cover of *Time* magazine. Surrounding her likeness are silhouetted images of McCardell's designs, photographed by former fashion model, Lisa Fonssagrives, later Mrs. Irving Penn. Courtesy Time, Inc.

Opposite:
Day dress. Cotton, c. 1955. Fashion Institute of Technology. 1972.9.1. "Parade Sauvage" by Fernand Léger. McCardell's cotton print day dress in fabric designed by the French artist.

liberal and varied interpretation that her

designs inspired in fashion editors and photographers was a key part of McCardell's success. Louise Dahl-Wolfe, one of this country's most celebrated female fashion photographers, and the less celebrated but equally talented Genevieve Naylor, were only two among many who were enchanted by McCardell's sleek, imaginative designs.

The collaboration and ensuing friendship between Claire McCardell and Louise Dahl-Wolfe was fostered by *Harper's Bazaar*. The legacy of this rich friendship is in the surviving photographs of their many collaborative efforts in which McCardell's designs were flawlessly interpreted and set into the pages of *Harper's Bazaar* via Dahl-Wolfe's masterful, straightforward photography. Years later, in her *Photographer's Scrapbook* (1984), Louise Dahl-Wolfe's autobiographical sketch of her life and career in fashion, the photographer spoke of McCardell as one of her "favorite American fashion designers." Dahl-Wolfe and McCardell shared an uncanny unity of vision and artistic calling; in spirit they were both messengers of a new minimalist modernity, promoting the healthy, outdoorsy good looks of an all-American kind of beauty over the painfully refined glamour-girl looks of the period. Patently disinterested in styles that oppressed the female form, McCardell's comfort-first clothes were a perfect complement to Dahl-Wolfe's no-nonsense tribute to sporty American women. Photographing often in naturally lit outdoor settings, Dahl-Wolfe removed female beauty from the decorative, conspicuously luxurious settings often associated with high fashion.

Besides working together, the two women spent occasional weekends and holidays together in Frenchtown, New Jersey, where McCardell had a farmhouse and Dahl-Wolfe and her husband had a vacation home nearby. They often shared time away from New York with a small circle of intimate industry friends, including fashion editor Sally Kirkland, friend and neighbor Peg Le Boutillier, and fashion designer Vera Maxwell. With no telephone, and well out of reach of the busy pace of Manhattan, McCardell and her fashion cartel would dream up fashion shoots, shop the local farmer's markets, and, in her hours of repose, the designer was even known to try her hand at painting still lifes. Though Claire was renowned for her cooking skills and her famous garlic stews, when asked to describe McCardell's oil paintings, a family friend paused, then smiled and replied, "Claire made such lovely clothes. . . ."

In addition to her intimacy with Dahl-Wolfe, McCardell enjoyed a personable and genuine rapport with a surprisingly large number of New York's fashion writers and public relations figures. But despite New York's importance as America's fashion capital, it was perhaps Claire's frequent trips to other major cities and small towns in the Midwest, South, and California that encouraged and sustained the designer's regional press coverage. By the late 1940s, whenever a new McCardell look was being unveiled or promoted, Claire was traveling extensively to keep up with a regular schedule of public appearances, store visits, and lectures at educational institutions

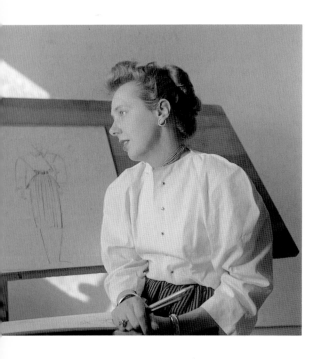

Portrait of Claire McCardell by her friend Louise Dahl-Wolfe. 1943. Center for Creative Photography. University of Arizona

In her own idiosyncratic way, McCardell often dressed herself in unlikely combinations, which nevertheless suited her purpose. Seen here at her farmhouse in Frenchtown in 1946, she wears a cycling shirt, a wool skirt, and the apron from her 1941 Kitchen Dinner dress. Photo, Toni Frissell, 1946

McCardell in the kitchen of her farmhouse in Frenchtown, New Jersey, in the mid-1940s.

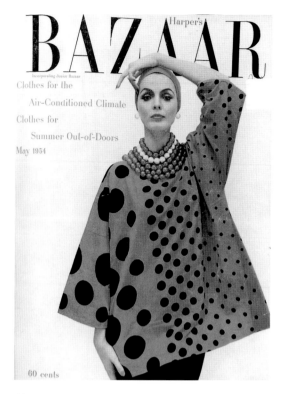

Harper's
BAZAAR
Incorporating Junior Bazaar

Clothes for the
Air-Conditioned Climate
Clothes for
Summer Out-of-Doors
May 1954

60 cents

Above:
McCardell's "T-square" top, inspired by her architect
husband's drafting tools, looked as appealing on the cover
of *Harper's Bazaar* as it did in the Fuller Brush catalogue.
Photo, Richard Avedon, for *Harper's Bazaar*, 1954

Opposite:
Day dress. Wool knit. c. 1950. Fashion Institute of
Technology. Gift of Sally Kirkland. 76.33.35
Among working women, McCardell was championed as
the designer of the "wear anywhere" dresses.

and among special-interest groups. Crossing the country by plane to promote her collections (and always with only one McCardell-packed suitcase full of separates), the increasingly famous designer met face-to-face with the American women whom she had been dressing for more than a decade.

Though Claire also reached the American public by radio and, by the 1950s, had appeared in promotional television spots and on talk shows, the informal meetings at trunk shows and ladies' luncheons formed an integral part of McCardell's publicity campaign, and fostered a loyal following for the down-to-earth New York designer. Though she had always designed first for herself, McCardell believed that meeting and speaking about clothes with women from all over America was the second most important influence on her collections.

Behind the scenes, fashion insiders who knew Claire McCardell personally appreciated her self-derived, truth-in-principle approach to fashion: the clothes she sold were the clothes she herself wore. The young women working in the fashion industry eagerly promoted McCardell's designs. They found Claire's looks fresh, relevant, and exciting, and had grown to respect her for her daring, even risky, takes on moderately priced American sportswear. What was more, Townley's warm, easygoing designer was always willing to lend samples for a fashion shoot or make up a "one-off" idea to help an editor or stylist fill a particular niche in a story or even for their own wardrobe or a special event. For these fashionable young women, who were expected to look as chic as the magazines they represented, McCardell's affordable, "no price look" went a long way. One could purchase a McCardell outfit on a working woman's salary, without even so much as hinting at its relatively low price, given the impeccable cut, sleek lines and highly sophisticated styling of the clothes. Bernadine Morris of the *New York Times*, a devout McCardell enthusiast as well as one of America's most authoritative fashion writers, remembers that she bought her first Claire McCardell in the early 1950s with her first paycheck from *Women's Wear Daily*—"they were both $55."[1]

In the closets of more than a few American women "Claire McCardell Clothes" hung alongside dresses by other designers costing literally ten times as much. One such was Slim Keith, the wife of Hollywood mogul Howard Hawks, who could easily afford to buy clothing from any designer she wanted. The epitome of reductive elegance and throw-away chic in the heyday of Hollywood's heavily made-up glamour girls, Slim Keith's look was refreshing: capri pants, black jersey separates, T-strap leather sandals, with her long, unstyled hair pulled back in a loose ponytail. Prone to restrained, often man-tailored looks, Keith was not only a perfect candidate for a Claire McCardell model, she was able to spot them for other talents: it was Slim Keith who first brought McCardell's young model, Lauren Bacall, to the attention of her film director–husband, thus launching the career of yet another casually all-American beauty by getting Bacall her first film role opposite Humphrey Bogart in *To Have and Have Not*.

Above: Top-stitched cotton twill sheath dress with slash pockets. Jean Patchett, Alhambra, Spain
Inexpensive and elegant: this credo defined McCardell and helped launch her in the world of working women. Photo, Louise Dahl-Wolfe, for *Harper's Bazaar*, 1953. Center for Creative Photography, University of Arizona

Opposite: Rayon crepe day dress with contrasting ties and slash pockets. This was from McCardell's last collection. Photo, Louise Dahl-Wolfe, for *Harper's Bazaar*, 1958. Center for Creative Photography, University of Arizona

Above: Evening dress. Cotton, 1954. Fashion Institute of Technology. Gift of Sally Kirkland, 76.33.16
Peg LeBoutillier (whose father owned Best & Co.) remarked on McCardell's knack for designing style at a moderate price.

Opposite, left to right: Evening dress. Nylon, c. 1950. Gift of Adrian McCardell, 72.61.182; Evening dress with self-wrap ties. Nylon. Gift of Adrian McCardell, 72.61.182. Both, Fashion Institute of Technology
McCardell had long been accustomed to scouring the fabric mills for unusual possibilities. These two evening dresses were cut from nylon tricot typically used for the lingerie market. Delicately draped in the manner of the Empress Josephine, McCardell's subtly sexy evening wear designs were as innovative as they were alluring and could hold their own against dresses costing ten times as much.

Another A-list McCardell fan was Babe Paley, born Barbara Cushing, a junior editor at *Vogue* who wore McCardell from her earliest days at the typewriter right through her years as one New York's most glamorous hostesses. In keeping with McCardell's own spirit of stylish contradiction, she was even known to liven up Claire's jersey separates (of which she owned many) with jewels from Harry Winston or Cartier (of which she owned even more). A regular on Eleanor Lambert's list of best-dressed women, Babe Paley remained a McCardell fan throughout her life.

Be they journalists, college girls, suburban mothers, fashion editors, Hollywood starlets, society wives, or even fashion models, it was precisely these progressive young women who best understood McCardell's modernizing influence on American fashion and followed McCardell's work and career with what one source close to McCardell once described as "a cultlike devotion." Peg Le Boutillier, a close personal friend of Claire's, whose father owned Best & Co., described McCardell's designs as being "about 3 years ahead of time," adding that her "exciting talent is designing haute couture that wholesales from $10.95 to $22.00."[2]

In what appears to have been prepared as some sort of press release (though Eleanor Lambert handled most of Townley's public relations), Le Boutillier offers an encapsulated glimpse of McCardell's relevance to American fashion: "Claire McCardell is a cult to many buyers who buy for the masses, and a cult to many fashion leaders who buy for individuality and chic. What designer, either before or after McCardell, can be said to have fit the bill for both of these clients?"[3]

By the late 1940s, nearly every major manufacturer of housewares, appliances, and cleaning products had accurately targeted American women as the consumer who wielded the most buying power. In an attempt to seduce women back into the kitchen in order to make jobs available for the men who were returning from the war, the American marketplace was flooded with all manner of sleekly designed, color-coordinated kitchen appliances and gadgets which promptly became as much an indicator of feminine appeal as the clothes women chose to wear. Claire's widespread recognition began to attract a variety of firms hoping to market their goods with the McCardell seal of approval, which eventually led to an amazing array of licensing arrangements. Having become one of the first American sportswear designers to gain such celebrated fame under her own name, McCardell unwittingly became a marketable role model for postwar American women: Claire's independently gained success was just the image America wanted to promote. At the height of her career, McCardell had either designed for or lent her name to no less than a dozen products and manufacturers.

In addition to a longstanding affiliation with Capezio, in the 1940s McCardell and Klein negotiated a licensing agreement to design a line of costume jewelry that was produced by Accessocraft and marketed under McCardell's name; also around this time McCardell had licensed commercial patterns of her designs for home sewers. Following that, Claire

"Cool-Ray" sun veil designed by McCardell.
Photo, John Engstead, 1958. Courtesy *Vogue*

McCardell gloves were signed to J. Rubin & Co., and Claire McCardell paper dolls became available under the auspices of Claire McCardell Enterprises, a separate corporation that controlled licensing agreements and was jointly owned by Claire and Adolph Klein. By the mid-1950s sunglasses, marketed as "Sunspecs by Claire McCardell," became available and were being featured in national advertisements. Shortly thereafter, a perfume formula ("White Sash by Claire McCardell") was in the works, complete with a McCardell-designed flip-top package covered with Claire's signature blue-lined graph paper that she had been using for years on hang tags and stationery. As if reminding us that Claire had been in Paris in 1927, the bottle for "White Sash" (which was never completed for distribution) bears a striking resemblance to Coco Chanel's original No. 5 flagon.

A large portion of Townley's advertising was done in conjunction with the fabric mills that supplied the designer with her seasonal fabrics. In the early days of co-op, or shared expense, advertising, McCardell and Klein shrewdly identified this as an inexpensive way to obtain publicity, and as Claire's reputation grew, the mills and manufacturers themselves (such as Enkya Rayons and Miron Woolens) became more than willing to sponsor the ad space in exchange for the celebrated designer's endorsement of their goods. As a result, McCardell eventually came to exercise considerable influence over domestic fabric suppliers as to color and weave, and eagerly encouraged the American mills to explore the possibilities of experimental synthetics that had begun to appear on the market.

Given McCardell's public esteem and increasing popularity among American women, the designer was asked to endorse products ranging from the fashion related to others more prosaic: playing cards, kitchen counters, composite kitchen fixtures, Fuller Brush cleaning products, even white bread! The patriotic designer's indomitable belief in American industry was probably responsible for attracting lucrative licensing agreements with American automobile manufacturers such as Chrysler, Kaiser, and Chevrolet. Later, in the mid-1950s, Claire McCardell lent her name and image to the Clairol Corporation in conjunction with advertisements endorsing hair color. At one point, she was even asked to create a dress for an elephant rider who was performing in a traveling circus. In 1952, Claire wrote to her stepson, John Harris, that when she had been to the circus to see "the lady in question in action all the animals behaved badly and the acrobats missed their cues!" Notwithstanding, McCardell did get a better sense of the costume needed for the elephant rider.

There was another pivotal factor contributing to Claire McCardell's meteoric rise in the media in the early 1950s, and that was her publicist, Eleanor Lambert. A veritable pioneer in fashion networking and public relations since the 1930s, Lambert's high-profile social access and shrewd business sense helped refine McCardell's client list and public image. Lambert was largely responsible for bringing Claire McCardell, a mid-market American designer, the media attention and social recognition

The Claire McCardell paper dolls, one of the designer's first licensed products, recall the paper dolls that McCardell made as a girl in the attic of her family home.

Factice of White Sash by Claire McCardell. Circa 1956

usually reserved for French couturiers. Though she once commented that Claire designed sophisticated sportswear with the charm of the "American peasant," with Lambert's skill behind her Claire McCardell Clothes came to be spoken of at the tables of international society women who would otherwise never think to mention, let alone wear an off-the-rack dress.[4] A perfect example of the social cross-pollination that Lambert could bring about is apparent in a surviving letter from screen star Joan Crawford thanking Lambert for the "beautiful Claire McCardell sunglasses," and saying how she hoped one day to meet the designer in person.

Besides moving McCardell's name and image up the New York social ladder, Lambert supplied the designer with brilliantly worded press releases, and arranged radio interviews and occasional television appearances. This far into her career, with so many successes behind her, McCardell slowly began to overcome her previous aversion to public speaking. The formerly shy girl who grew up below the Mason-Dixon line was beginning to show another side. The experienced, naturally poised fashion visionary soon began to charm radio and television audiences and interviewers alike with her fresh candor and easy, even-keeled Southern manner.

McCardell seemed to be drawing upon an inexhaustible well of innovative, new concepts in American fashion. Clearly, an important and increasingly visible American design force was emerging, and fashion writers and pop culture critics (including feminist Betty Friedan, who referred to McCardell in the 1950s as "the girl who defied Dior") were well aware of it even as it was happening. Barbara Scott Fisher of the *Christian Science Monitor* wrote a feature story on McCardell and the designer's 1944 summer line. Fisher was fascinated by Claire's left-of-center designs and described McCardell's approach to dress construction by saying that it was "as though she took hold of the practical, basic idea in what she desired to create, then said it with scissors in the shortest and least involved manner."

Since the end of the war, Claire's public image was regularly reinforced by the impressive number of press awards and honors that she received for her daring, adventurous designs. McCardell was being honored both by the magazines that featured her designs and the stores that sold them. The 1943 *Mademoiselle* Merit Award was presented to Claire for having "batted out a brilliant series of firsts," and "whose triumph as a designer may be defined as flair-at-a-price: a unique talent for applying *haute couture* wit to the mass-production dress." The designer's spirited ability to work around wartime shortages was then commended, adding that many of McCardell's designs prove that "L-85 is no handicap to true creative ability."

The next year, in 1944, *Life* ran a cover story on America's ten most noteworthy designers, and Claire was featured alongside her previous employer, Hattie Carnegie. McCardell also received the Golden Thimble Award for her outstanding design talents in 1946. From the late 1940s, Claire seemed to be nominated, if not chosen, for nearly every press and

Far left: Day dress. Cotton, c. 1949. Fashion Institute of Technology. Gift of Hood College, 96.61.7
The archetypal McCardell shirtwaist, and one of the designer's most popular sellers. Unfortunately, the shirtwaist became so associated with McCardell that it gave the impression—wrongly—that she catered mostly to suburban housewives.

Near left: Hostess dress. Wool, c. 1950. Fashion Institute of Technology. Gift of Adrian McCardell, 72.61.114
Claire's plaid wool wrap-waisted hostess dress was the perfect at-home dinner dress for the sophisticated suburbanite. With their smartly mitered stripes and self-tailored waistlines, these McCardell standards sold in the hundreds of thousands.

Claire McCardell in her
"futuristic dress" cut only
of triangles. In prior
publications, this photo of
the designer was erroneously
attributed to John Rawlings.
Photo. Erwin Blumenfeld.
1945. Courtesy *Vogue*

fashion-related honor, including being elected as chairman at the Fashion Group and asked to serve on the advisory board of the Metropolitan Museum of Art's Costume Institute in New York.

In 1945, just as American fashion had begun to make its presence felt, a controversial exhibition at New York's Museum of Modern Art was launched. "Are Clothes Modern?" was based on historian Bernard Rudofsky's published inquiry into fashion and its inability to keep stride with technology and evolving human lifestyles. Citing the absurdity of past fashions such as the bustle and contemporary trends such as high heels, the show included one text panel that denounced contemporary designers for not knowing "any better way of using a fabric than cutting it to pieces," and went on to urge that "Instead of turning out simulated tailor-made clothes, industry could produce intelligent garments, designed for machine production." This generalization may have caused unrest among more than a few New York dressmakers, but there remained one American designer who provided a glitch in the show's thesis. Three of McCardell's most minimal, pared-down designs were displayed, as was an original drawing of hers. The accompanying wall label offered faint praise: "True innovation in design is practically restricted to play clothes, a category of dress, which in time, may be the starting point for the creating of a genuine contemporary apparel." Inevitably, Claire McCardell was included in the lineup, but without the acknowledgment that McCardell had been designing modern, streamlined clothing specifically for the mass-production market since the 1930s.

The exhibition dealt a swift blow to the perceived importance of contemporary designers. In an effort to quell disgruntled rumblings from the

By the early 1950s, McCardell had attracted licenses for
a number of accessories, including sunglasses, jewelry, shoes,
gloves, and hats. The model at rear center wears a short leather
skirt, another McCardell first. Photo, Mark Shaw, 1954

Model Sunny Harnett in McCardell's South American
inspired off-the-shoulder hostess dress, 1952.

industry, *Vogue* ran a response in February of 1946, exclaiming that "definitively, Yes!" clothing was modern, and, in addition to featuring a full-page photo of Claire McCardell in her future dress—cut all from triangles—there was an argument explaining why fashion was modern. That both factions cited McCardell (albeit one rather begrudgingly) as fashion's indisputable messenger of modernity is indicative of the clout McCardell's progressive designs carried with contemporary chroniclers of popular culture.

In 1946, Claire, along with other design professionals (among them Raymond Loewy and Elsa Schiaparelli), began volunteering to serve as a critic in the fashion design department at Parsons School of Design. Frank Rizzo, then a design student (who later went on to become the chairman of the fashion design department at Parsons), was part of McCardell's advisory group back in the early 1950s, and remembers that "Claire was by far the most fun . . . she really let us get creative." Reminiscing about the designer herself, Rizzo added that "there was something wonderfully offbeat, even funky about Claire . . . in a way that was almost hard to describe." Rizzo concluded, "If it hadn't been the 1950s, I'd say she had a bit of the hippie in her!"[5]

Remembering Claire's difficulties in remaining focused while she had been a student at Parsons, one of McCardell's family members mused that working with the young, aspiring designers "was probably the only circumstance under which Claire would ever have willingly returned to a classroom!"[6] But despite her previous impatience, McCardell strongly believed in supporting formal education and knew from experience that for those seeking a future in the design world, a solid familiarity with clothing construction was the necessary point of departure. Always managing to find time in her increasingly busy work schedule, McCardell continued working with students at Parsons on and off throughout her lifetime.

In 1948, American retail magnate Stanley Marcus presented Claire with the Neiman-Marcus Award for "her refreshing creative spirit and her completely American approach toward fashion." In a thoughtful, respectful address, Marcus characterized McCardell as being "the master of the line, never a slave to the sequin," and referred to Claire as "one of the few truly creative designers this country has produced, borrowing nothing from other designers. She is to America what Vionnet was, and now Grès is, to France."[7]

In 1950, McCardell became the first fashion designer to be honored by the Women's National Press Club, and was saluted for her "famous casuals—favorites with career women and 'the typical American girl,'" as well as "her belief that clothes are made to be lived in and therefore should be comfortable." Standing alongside famed dancer Martha Graham and actress Olivia de Havilland, McCardell was presented this distinguished honor by President Harry S. Truman. She cherished this award perhaps more than any other. Having consistently championed American style and resisted the trend for Eurocentric taste, McCardell had earned the recognition that most appropriately reflected her mission—endorsement of American achievement, and a place among women of her time who were actively expanding and redefining the roles of contemporary American women. Having become the first American fashion designer to have been so honored, McCardell felt that this award symbolized a new pride in American fashion while pointing toward the continued elevation of America's mass-production standards she had long fought to bring about.

Claire's stepdaughter, Elizabeth Harris, remembers the day that McCardell was honored by President Truman. For most people such an honor would have been made much of at home, but the bashful designer had her own way of handling such matters: "It was a Saturday," Harris remembers, "and we were supposed to go to the farmhouse, but Mumsy [as the Harris children called Claire] had her city clothes on. She said she had some business to take care of and would be back the next day—that we would leave then. It was only by accident that we heard on the radio that she had slipped out to receive an award from the President of the United States!"[8]

Nearly ten years after the show at the Museum of Modern Art, Claire's designs once again ended up back on display in an exhibition. This time, however, McCardell was given far more than an honorable mention for her contribution to the modern American mode of dressing. In April of 1953, the Frank Perls Gallery in Beverly Hills launched a retrospective exhibition of twenty years of Claire McCardell's designs that *Look* magazine pointed out was probably the first one-person show where clothing was exhibited as a work of art. In a stark white room, two decades of McCardell's designs were displayed on wire forms which were suspended from chains attached to the ceiling and floor.

That a modern art gallery (whose owner had been unknown to McCardell) would install a retrospective exhibition of a living fashion designer's work lends insight into the respect McCardell's design genius had achieved beyond the fashion world. The conception of "fashion as art" had not been fully developed since the widely publicized Schiaparelli collections of the 1930s, which incorporated the work of Surrealist artists including Salvador Dalí. By contrast to Schiaparelli, who designed some of her imaginative creations in conjunction with renowned painters, McCardell's work did not incorporate the application of another artist's visual decoration. What Frank Perls saw, and what America had long recognized, was the pure design genius inherent in McCardell's entirely undecorated visions of women's clothing—the design of the garment itself, its cut, its functionality—its "McCardellism." Believing only in that which withstood constant erasure, Claire McCardell had mastered the art of design.

Also in 1953, Stanley Marcus, a longtime McCardell supporter (who, incidentally, had written the copy for the Perls gallery's invitation), honored the designer by installing a corresponding mini exhibition in Neiman-Marcus stores across the country. Not to be outdone, Lord & Taylor also dedicated its

Ensemble, consisting of jacket, pants, and short boots. Cotton twill, wool jersey, 1950s. Fashion Institute of Technology. Gift of Mr. and Mrs. Adrian McCardell, 72.61.60ABCD.

The polished cotton and wool jersey pants with matching boots look ahead to the sleek mod looks of the 1960s.

Day dress (front and rear views). Cotton pique, 1958. Fashion Institute of Technology. Gift of Hood College, 96.61.4

Claire McCardell's last collections were created with the assistance of Mildred Orrick. Dating from 1958, this cotton pique top-stitched day dress draws heavily on the increasingly geometric influences that McCardell began to favor toward the end of her career.

entire Fifth Avenue window front as well as an in-store exhibition to Claire McCardell, in honor of the designer's past twenty years of continued and dedicated contributions to American fashion. In 1953, it seemed that the American fashion industry bowed to Claire McCardell.

In 1955, *Life* ran a fashion editorial featuring fabrics designed by several important European painters including Marc Chagall, Pablo Picasso, Fernand Léger, Joan Miró, and Raoul Dufy. Working on the article in the south of France with her old friend and *Life*'s fashion editor Sally Kirkland, McCardell designed a wardrobe of separates and dress ensembles from fabrics printed with works by these various artists. Claire's fame had long since spread overseas, but for an American designer to command the attention of a lineup of internationally renowned painters was not only remarkable, it was unprecedented. The effect this *Life* article had on Claire's reputation can only be imagined. But once again, Claire McCardell had transcended all expectation of fashion, this time by cutting dresses from humble cottons printed by artists whose canvases literally sold for small fortunes.

Above: In 1955, McCardell was honored by the Women's National Press Club and received an award from President Harry S. Truman. Left to right: Martha Graham, dancer; Dorothy Fosdick, government; Dr. Pearl Wanamaker, education; Margaret Truman; President Truman; Mrs. Truman; Olivia De Havilland, actress; Dr. Mildred Rebstock, science; and Claire McCardell, designer. Photo, Paul Schmeck, *Washington Post*, 1953

In 1953, the Frank Perls Gallery in Beverly Hills launched a one-person retrospective of McCardell's designs between 1933 and 1953. *Look* magazine. Courtesy of the Historical Society of Frederick County, Inc.

As seen in Chagall's studio, the model's dress was the
result of a collaboration between Marc Chagall and
McCardell. Photo, Mark Shaw, for *Life* magazine, 1955

Picasso, among other artists, worked with McCardell
to develop textiles based on his work. Here, Picasso in
his Cannes studio jests with famed French model Bettina,
who wears a Picasso/McCardell print ensemble.
Photo, Mark Shaw, for *Life* magazine, 1955

While McCardell's relationship with the media unquestionably contributed to her overwhelming commercial success, the designer herself had the opportunity to return the favor when in 1954 she was asked by Time, Inc., to become part of an advisory panel to create a new magazine. The result was *Sports Illustrated*. In an insert for the magazine's first issue, McCardell wrote a brief essay with the provocative title, "Women Are What They Wear." (The insert cover showed a starkly modern wire dress form.)

> Sports clothes changed our lives because they changed our thinking about clothes. Perhaps they, more than anything else, made us independent women. In the days of dependent women—fainting women—delicate flowers—laced to breathless beauty—a girl couldn't cross the street without help. Her mission in life was to look beautiful and seductive while the men took care of the world's problems. Today women can share the problems (and possibly help with them) partly because of their new found freedom from clothes.

Two years later, after the fledgling publication was well on its way to becoming established, McCardell was honored by *Sports Illustrated* and presented with the American Sportswear Design Award.

Perhaps Claire's most far-reaching media triumph had come the year before, in May of 1955, when she became one of only three fashion designers ever to make the cover of *Time* magazine. On a cover flanked by renderings of youthful models wearing her designs, McCardell, then fifty years old, lived up to writer Osborne Elliott's observation that the designer of young fashions was still her own best model. More than merely identifying McCardell's status as a fashion trendsetter or as an old-fashioned American success story, the *Time* piece rightly identified McCardell's unique position as a catalyst in the evolution of American fashion.

Claire's own book, *What Shall I Wear?* was published the next year, in 1956. Co-written with Edith Heal and subtitled "The What, Where, When and How Much of Fashion," McCardell's book was described in one review as "a lyrical journey through the fashion philosophy of Claire McCardell," and is full of clever anecdotes and explanations about the fickle nature of fashion. In it, McCardell takes the reader on a shelf-by-shelf tour of her own closet and dispels many of fashion's most imperious myths while encouraging women to take stock of their sense of adventure as well as their wardrobe. The book's perspective is significant in that it addresses the role of fashion in McCardell's own life as opposed to her role as a designer of contemporary fashion. There was even a pullout list of "McCardellisms"—defined by Claire as "a glossary of terms which speak to me of fashion . . . and haven't very much to do with Webster."

Despite the fact that *What Shall I Wear?* reflects many of McCardell's common-sense ideas about accessories, dressing on a tight budget, and the

importance of not being upstaged by one's own clothes, the book was practically ghostwritten by Edith Heal, and therefore is not an entirely accurate take on McCardell's own fashion ideology. More of a McCardell product than a McCardell manifesto, *What Shall I Wear?* should be regarded with this in mind when formulating an opinion of Claire McCardell's design philosophies.

During the preparation of the manuscript for *What Shall I Wear?*, Edith Heal was simultaneously working on a book titled *The Young Executive's Wife: You and Your Husband's Job* — a guidebook published in 1958 of tips on how to become a pretty, husband-pleasing corporate wife. It's no coincidence that Claire's own book is likewise replete with housewifely hints and advice on dressing to impress neighbors when dropping off one's husband at the train station or when being scrutinized by the female competition at the grocery store. Not only were these situations not part of McCardell's own life, they were not part of the independent McCardell mindset: nothing in Claire McCardell's world suggested a tolerance for being dismissed as a decorative accessory for her husband. Far from it. Claire's stepdaughter remembers that "Claire was a feminist long before we had a name for them." But in 1956, feminism was a hard sell in fashion while Heal's vision of the docile, man-pleasing executive wife really was more in keeping with the June Cleaver/Doris Day types of women who were popular at the time. As it was in Townley's best interest that *What Shall I Wear?* be well reviewed, Heal was entrusted to do more than just put the finishing touches on the book.

McCardell's brother, Robert, willingly concedes that *What Shall I Wear?* was a "highly collaborative effort,"[9] and another brother, Adrian, euphemistically acknowledged that his sister was "long on dresses, but short on words."[10] Moreover, in *What Shall I Wear?* the quirky, rebellious suggestions that are unmistakably Claire's are easily recognized: "I like my furs to peek out as linings or to look kind of moth-eaten and raggedy or to be quite bold."[11] Conversely, how likely is it that a woman known to ski in a cheetah fur jacket with stainless steel industrial clips would caution other women that "your major rule should be 'conservative.' . . . You don't want heads to turn!"[12]

Despite the fact that Claire McCardell's designs and fashion philosophies received a substantial amount of media coverage throughout her lifetime, McCardell's work is often remembered in surprisingly limited scope. By far the most common misconception—due in large part to *What Shall I Wear?* and also perhaps because of her various commercial endorsements—is that Claire McCardell designed mainly for suburban housewives. Undeniably, a large share of McCardell's market stemmed from upper-middle-class women who were keen on the utilitarian but still stylish appeal of Claire's wash-and-wear shirtwaist dresses and utilitarian designs. However, to categorize Claire McCardell as a designer for the at-home suburban set would be as inaccurate as describing Calvin Klein as a designer of blue jeans. If McCardell is remembered for her middle-class customer appeal, it's because her "bread-and-butter" dresses received widespread publicity, sold well, and were in synch with popular images of contemporary women in the media during the late 1940s and 1950s. But there were her more adventurous and unique designs: McCardell's redwood bark jump suits (1943), yard-long green felt elf hats (1945), and "indecently bare" bathing suits. What was chic along the sophisticated South Fork shores of Long Island or among the "in set" at Vassar College often went unseen by a large portion of the Midwestern market sweep that made up McCardell's unusually diverse clientele. With this in mind, it is not surprising that the dresses chosen for McCardell's national advertisements were those that Townley's owners felt exhibited the broadest possible market appeal, those they hoped would prove to be the most "wearable" and therefore commercially successful. Consequently, historic perceptions of McCardell's clothes are informed by her most publicized and most popular designs which, arguably, were not always her most important ones.

This skewed perception of McCardell's extensive design repertoire is apparent in *Radical by Design*, Bettina Berch's biography of American fashion designer Elizabeth Hawes. In an otherwise insightful and well-researched book about one of McCardell's early competitors, Berch errs with her simplistic contrast of Hawes and McCardell by casting McCardell into the role of a corporate-backed "suburban" fashion stylist, while suggesting that Hawes was America's only truly artistic, free-thinking fashion innovator who was martyred upon the cross of bottom-line capitalism. Though Elizabeth Hawes may have been a more intellectual designer than Claire McCardell, McCardell was more keenly tuned into what the majority of American women wanted to wear. It was this awareness, and the clothes which reflected it that sold America on Claire McCardell Clothes, and not, as Berch suggests, a "sympathetic clothing manufacturer . . . and a businessman husband."[13] Moreover, Berch overlooks that McCardell succeeded in her efforts to bring good design to the American public at affordable prices, while Hawes's own design-for-the-masses concepts proved unsuccessful in the commercial ready-to-wear market.

Despite these discrepancies, Elizabeth Hawes and Claire McCardell actually shared many relevant but less immediately noticeable traits. Hawes, like McCardell, had learned the techniques of the Parisian couture and, again like Claire, throughout her lifetime remained wary of what she called "The French Legend." She, too, repeatedly refused to accept that America, with such advanced mass-production technology already in place, could not manage to produce elegant, tasteful clothes for all within its borders. Additionally, Hawes received a lot of press coverage for her highly original, often sensational designs to which, again like McCardell, she assigned rather outrageous names. However, in 1934, *Vogue* editor Edna Woolman Chase told her Paris correspondent Bettina Ballard (who was wearing a pink tweed Elizabeth Hawes suit when the conversation took place), that she thought Hawes was "better at making publicity than clothes"—an accusation that was never to shadow the career of Claire McCardell.[14]

"Suburban" or not, McCardell's designs had become popular among the increasingly prevalent twenty- to thirtysomething commuter crowd. By providing versatile, sensibly cut feminine clothes to this steadily growing segment of the American population, McCardell had captured yet another portion of the market that would ultimately form a substantial part of her following. With her unparalleled diversity increasingly reflected in her advertising—day wear, play clothes, ski parkas, tennis clothes, and evening gowns—by the late 1940s McCardell had firmly established her reputation as America's only designer creating appropriate clothing for nearly every occasion. But plain or dressy, each of the designer's looks proved to be as distinctively "McCardell" as the next: the calico Kitchen Dinner dress with matching apron for meals prepared at home was just as characteristically "McCardell" as the backless taffeta ensemble for black tie dinners.

In addition to her crowd-pleasing designs, by the 1950s Claire was becoming as innovative in business as she was in her approach to fashion. She was one of the first American designers to send her own house models along with the traveling trunk shows for buyers and their clients in department and specialty stores across the country. Claire chose showroom models who were about five feet, seven inches tall, long legged, lean, and a perfect size 10—in short, McCardell's exact measurements. She even instructed her most popular traveling muse, Betty Ann Brown, on how to walk with that slightly haughty McCardell slouch, always with hands in the ubiquitous McCardell pockets. In this way, the exacting designer was able to ensure that the clothes would not be worn by indifferent house models who might lack the understanding and enthusiasm of a seasoned McCardell recruit. The seemingly laid-back, casual gait that Claire taught her models was a thinly disguised but more stylized version of the shy designer's own retracting stance, which succeeded in lending the models an air of ease in perfect accord with the clothes they were wearing.

Fashion models weren't the only beautiful women wearing Claire McCardell's designs in the 1950s. Having made more than a few trips to Los Angeles, McCardell was known by and interacted with several Hollywood personalities who wore her clothes, including such stars as Katharine Hepburn, Rosalind Russell, and Rita Hayworth. On one trip to Los Angeles, McCardell met Edith Head, one of the movies' most successful and influential costume designers. Head created glamorous designs for starlets both on and off camera and soon became a personal friend of Claire's. Head and McCardell lunched, talked fashion, and visited museums together when business brought one of them into the other's sphere. Though Claire was not impressed by movie stars, she had been thrilled to learn that during the exhibition at the Perls Gallery in Beverly Hills Greta Garbo had asked permission to bring her dressmaker in to copy Claire's black jersey separates—which McCardell had designed nearly twenty years before and had been wearing herself ever since.

In the autumn of 1957, at the height of her career, and without warning of any kind, Claire McCardell was diagnosed with cancer. Despite more than six months of intensive treatment, by January of the next year, the fifty-two-year-old designer was becoming increasingly ill. True to her rebellious nature, Claire defied her doctors' orders not to return to Townley to finish her last two collections, and despite having collapsed more than once on the job, she telephoned from the hospital for a limousine to pick her up and deliver her to her Seventh Avenue workrooms. As her condition worsened, Adolph Klein attempted to comply with McCardell's wish to complete her last collection for the coming year by asking Mildred Orrick, Claire's long-time friend since their days together at Parsons, to help the ailing designer, who was by then confined to the hospital.

In January of 1958, with barely enough strength to stand, McCardell, with the help of Mildred Orrick, dressed in her favorite red denim suit and slipped past her nurses to attend the last showing of her clothes at the Pierre Hotel. Columnist Dorothy Parnell, among those who knew of McCardell's illness, was truly surprised to see Claire, and was deeply moved to hear McCardell say with a weak smile that the best friends she had in her career had been "the newspaper women—I wouldn't miss seeing them for anything." [15]

At that last show, McCardell made her way to the runway to wave to the throngs of loyal followers who had heard that it would be the renowned designer's last collection, where she was greeted with a standing ovation. McCardell returned to the hospital that evening determined to continue working from her bed, but the cancer was too far advanced.

Though the majority of the sketches for Townley's final 1958 seasons are in Mildred Orrick's hand, more than a few are altered or drawn over in the distinctive and recognizably witty hand of America's most American designer, who, up until her death on March 22nd of that year, had insisted on "making them better."

Epilogue: Claire-voyant

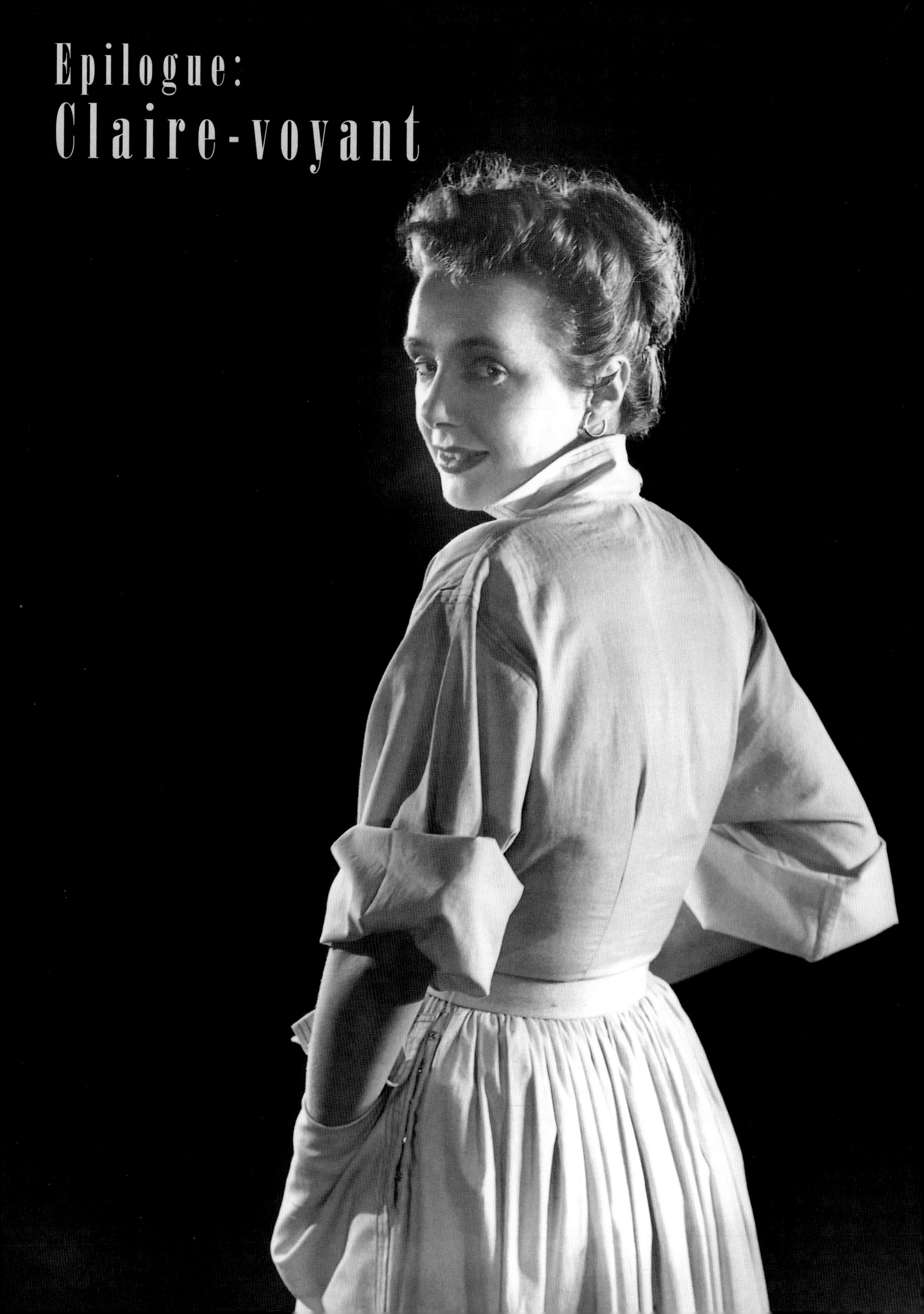

She was a pioneer of minimalism, an innovator of modernism, and

throughout her short but influential career Claire McCardell provided women with designs that stressed comfort, practicality, and integrity. Hers is a design message that has endured over the four decades since her early death. The foundation of McCardell's efforts—practical separates and sportswear—have become dominant themes in the American woman's wardrobe. For McCardell, it was the application of a passion to design with her common sense and the understanding of what women really needed that helped popularize sportswear—and not just in America but throughout the world. Indeed, sportswear as we know it today has its conceptual roots in the so-called play clothes of Claire McCardell.

By mid-century, and especially around the time of World War II, women's lifestyles and social roles were changing; McCardell responded by putting America's mass-production capabilities into motion to create afford-able, easily cared for modern apparel. The Pop-over dress, complete with a matching kitchen mitt and orginally priced at $6.95, is just one example of her ingenuity and ever-present practicality. So too is the Monastic dress, with its adaptable waistline.

McCardell's influence is both specific and general. Her knits and multipiece separates ensembles have been adapted as silhouettes in the collections of American and European designers at literally every price point. Likewise, the popularity and ubiquity of denim for daywear since

Claire McCardell. Photo.
Wynn Richards, 1945

137

McCardell first designed with it has proven the relevance of one of her avant-garde themes. Denim, and with it cotton sailcloth, were born of necessity: concerned that many American women could not afford the care and cleaning bills usually associated with designer clothes, McCardell used these fabrics for her garments, thus ennobling even these humble weaves. Though she favored cottons and wool jersey, McCardell was one of the earliest supporters of what have become known as "high-tech" fabrics. Partial to rayon and elasticized fabrics long before they gained popular acceptance, McCardell looked beyond the immediate, intended use of these new and experimental fabrics.

Tributes to McCardell have come by way of exhibitions and the reintroduction of some of her most popular designs. In 1972, both the Los Angeles County Museum of Art and New York's Fashion Institute of Technology paid tribute to Claire McCardell's enduring relevance to the American fashion scene. Fifteen years later, Richard Martin and Harold Koda, then curators at the Fashion Institute of Technology, mounted "Three Women," an exhibition highlighting the design geniuses of Madeleine Vionnet, Claire McCardell, and Rei Kawakubo. Each woman had at some point in the twentieth century challenged perceptions of design and in doing so had made fashion history.

In the early 1980s, spurred by renewed interest in McCardell, Lord & Taylor reissued a line of McCardell-inspired dresses. Though Townley Frocks had closed its doors after its 1958 season, nearly thirty years later Claire's Pop-over and Monastic dresses (along with a host of familiar others) were once again back on the racks of Lord & Taylor's Fifth Avenue store. With labels reading "Inspired by Claire McCardell," the cotton plaids and jersey sheaths were proof of McCardell's staying power. Beyond pleasing those who remembered McCardell from her heyday, the new McCardell-inspired looks were selling to young women, many of whom were unaware that they were purchasing dresses originally designed as much as fifty years earlier.

More recently, in the fall of 1994, in celebration of the 75th anniversary of the New School, Parsons School of Design launched "Claire McCardell: Redefining Modernism," a retrospective exhibition in honor of one of their most distinguished alumna. On a cool December opening night, as the exhibition space filled to capacity and then began to spill out into the street, a tall, striking blonde breezed past the crowd and spun out of her black jersey cape, revealing a backless, floor-length silk halter dress that caused an involuntary pause among the group. It was Claire's sister-in-law, Sue. The dress was fifty-one years old.

Notes

Chapter 1. Small Town Girl

1. Francis Staley Smith, interview by Nancy Nolf, spring 1996.
2. Claire McCardell, untitled speech delivered when presented with the Coty Award, 1944, McCardell Family Archives.
3. Claire McCardell, handwritten preparatory notes for Coty speech, version 2, McCardell Family Archives.
4. Sally Kirkland, "Claire McCardell," *American Fashion*, ed. Sally Tomerlin Lee (New York: Quadrangle Books, 1975), 314.
5. Robert C. McCardell, interview by Nancy Nolf, 20 August 1997.
6. C. McCardell, untitled speech, 1.
7. Claire McCardell, *Women are What They Wear*, insert in *Sports Illustrated* (New York: Time, Inc., 1954), 2.
8. C. McCardell, untitled speech, 1.
9. Mildred Orrick, letter to Eleanore McCardell.
10. Valerie Steele, *Women of Fashion, Twentieth Century Designers* (New York: Rizzoli, 1991), 57.
11. Claire McCardell, *What Shall I Wear? The What, Where, When, and How Much of Fashion* (New York: Simon & Schuster, 1956), promotional insert.
12. C. McCardell, untitled speech and preparatory notes.
13. Joset Walker, letter to Claire McCardell.
14. Kirkland, "Claire McCardell," 219.
15. R. C. McCardell, interview by Nolf.
16. Elizabeth Harris, interview by Kohle Yohannan, 24 August 1997.
17. C. McCardell, untitled speech.
18. Osburn Elliott, "The American Look," *Time* 65 (May 2, 1955): 91.
19. C. McCardell, untitled speech.
20. Ibid.
21. Ibid.
22. Elliott, "The American Look," 86.
23. Helen F. Wulbern, "Designers of Today and Tomorrow," *Women's Wear Daily* (1940), McCardell Family Archives.
24. C. McCardell, untitled speech.

Chapter 2: Townley Frocks

1. Elliott, "The American Look," 89.
2. R. C. McCardell, interview by Nolf.
3. Betty Friedan, "The Gal Who Defied Dior," *Town Journal* (October 1955): 97.
4. Karen Gardner, "Claire McCardell: She founded the women's sportswear movement in American Fashion," *Frederick News Post* (March 4, 1991): C-1.
5. Kirkland, "Claire McCardell," 232.
6. Ibid.
7. Adrian C. McCardell, interview by Nancy Nolf, 25 August 1997.

Chapter 3: "Claire McCardell Clothes"

1. Elliott, "The American Look," 90.
2. Ibid.
3. Ibid.
4. Claire McCardell, handwritten desk notes, McCardell Family Archives.
5. Harry Friedman, letter to Adolph Klein, 1958, McCardell Family Archives.
6. Kirkland, "Claire McCardell," 239.
7. Friedan, "The Gal Who Defied Dior," 97.
8. Eugenia Sheppard, "Team of McCardell and Klein Turned Tide of U.S. Fashion," *Baltimore News American* (August 23, 1968), McCardell Family Archives.
9. C. McCardell, *What Shall I Wear?* 85.
10. C. McCardell, handwritten desk notes.
11. "Who's News and Why," n.p. (November 1954), McCardell Family Archives.
12. Citation presented to Claire McCardell when she won the Coty Award in 1942, McCardell Family Archives.
13. Kirkland, "Claire McCardell," 211.
14. Caroline Rennolds Milbank, *New York Fashion* (New York: Harry N. Abrams, 1989), 162.
15. John Harris, interview by Nancy Nolf, 19 August 1997.
16. Kirkland, "Claire McCardell," 283.

Chapter 4: The American Look

1. Kirkland, "Claire McCardell," 240.
2. Friedan, "The Gal Who Defied Dior," 98.
3. Kirkland, "Claire McCardell," 224.
4. Ibid., 243.
5. Alice Hughes, "Claire McCardell Wins Rare Honor," n.p. (May 7, 1955), McCardell Family Archives.
6. Blanch Krause, "Claire McCardell is Exponent of Younger Look," n.p. (May 8, 1955), McCardell Family Archives.
7. C. McCardell, *What Shall I Wear?* 156.
8. C. McCardell, handwritten notes.
9. Unidentified article, McCardell Family Archives.
10. C. McCardell, *What Shall I Wear?* 13.
11. Elizabeth Harris, interview by Kohle Yohannan, 17 August 1997.
12. Claire McCardell, "Wardrobe Futures," *Washington Star* (February 9, 1945), McCardell Family Archives.
13. Ibid.

Chapter 5: McCardell and the Media

1. Bernardine Morris, Parsons exhibition review, *New York Times* (December 1994), McCardell Family Archives.

2. Peg LeBoutillier, "The Cult of Claire McCardell," four-page unpublished document (n.d.), McCardell Family Archives.
3. Ibid.
4. Bettina Berch, *Radical by Design: The Life and Style of Elizabeth Hawes* (New York: E. P. Dutton, 1988), 75.
5. Frank Rizzo, interview by Kohle Yohannan, fall 1994.
6. A. C. McCardell, interview by Nolf.
7. "The Neiman-Marcus Awards for distinguished service in the field of fashion," Advertisement, *Women's Wear Daily* (September 7, 1948): 15, McCardell Family Archives.
8. E. Harris, interview by Yohannan.
9. R. C. McCardell, interview by Nolf, 27 August 1997.
10. A. C. McCardell, interview by Nolf
11. C. McCardell, *What Shall I Wear?* 64.
12. Ibid., 74.
13. Berch, *Radical by Design*, 75.
14. Bettina Ballard, *In My Fashion: An Intimate Memoir About People, Places and Events that Make Up the World of High Fashion* (New York: David McKay Company, 1960), 3.
15. Dorothy Parnell, "Have You Heard," *Milwaukee Sentinel* (March 26, 1958), McCardell Family Archives.

Chronology

1905

Born May 24 in Frederick, Maryland

1923

Graduates from Frederick High School

1923-25

Studies home economics at Hood College

1926

Enrolls in Costume Illustration and Costume Construction at the School of Fine and Applied Arts (now known as Parsons School of Design) in New York

1926-27

Studies for one year in Paris as part of the Parsons program, then returns to New York City

1928

Graduates from Parsons School of Design

1929

After a series of odd jobs, goes to work as an assistant for Robert Turk, an independent designer

1931

Follows Turk to Townley Frocks

1932

After Robert Turk is killed in a boating accident, finishes the fall line and upon its success is promoted to full designer status at Townley

1934

McCardell's first five-piece system of interchangeable separates

1935

Dark red striped muffler silk dinner dress and jacket; navy jersey halter top

1936

"Spaghetti" string ties on dresses

1937

Townley's first bathing suits designed by McCardell

Brass hooks and eyes begin to appear regularly in collection

Men's gray flannel used for jackets and pleated trousers

1938

Brown wool Monastic dress (first advertised by Best & Co. as the Nada Frock); floor-length tweed evening coats; harem pants; exercise suits

Goes to work for Hattie Carnegie when Townley Frocks closes. Creates a line called "Workshop Originals" for Carnegie; designs hats for Carnegie; noted for brown-and-ivory rayon striped dress with sweetheart neckline and crossover side-attached sashes

1939

Wins First Prize at the New York World's Fair for costume design.

1940

Attends last couture shows in Paris (for Carnegie)

Works for Win-Sum for several months, returns to work for Townley Frocks, which reopens under Adolph Klein Black jersey baby doll dress

1941

Kitchen Dinner dress; white jersey wedding dress with coif

1942

Blue denim Pop-over with oven mitt; checked silk bloomer playsuit; Superman hood

Receives citation from the American Fashion Critics Association for the Pop-over

1943

Diaper bathing suit; blue denim bareback; riveted look

Cover of *Life* magazine features leotards designed by McCardell

Wins the Coty American Fashion Critics First Prize Award for excellence in apparel design

Marries Irving Drought Harris

1944

Receives merit award from *Mademoiselle* magazine

Pedal pusher

Introduces Capezio ballet slippers

1945

"Are Clothes Modern?" exhibition opens, Museum of Modern Art, New York

Writes "Wardrobe Futures" for the *Washington Star* and predicts that skirts will get longer and fuller, shoulders less padded and more rounded

Calico beach kilts; empire bathing suit

1946

Receives Golden Thimble and is named one of the ten best designers of women's apparel in the United States in a poll of 50,000 retailers conducted by the Fashion Trades

Barrel bathing suit

1947

Christian Dior's "New Look"
Elastic bodice dresses; petticoats; elastic tube bathing suits; full circle skirts

1948

Receives Neiman-Marcus Award for Distinguished Service in the field of fashion

First fully pleated dress

1949

Accordion pleated heather gray jersey Monastic dress; bandana neckline

Named by *Life* magazine as one of the ten most noted American designers

1950

Honored by the Women's National Press Club and is presented with certificate of achievement by the President of the United States, Harry S. Truman

1951

Pyramid Pop-over

Hood College Alumnae Award

1952

Becomes a partner in Townley

Stringbean dress; plaid wrap-and-tie Pop-over

1953

The Frank Perls Gallery in Beverly Hills launches a twenty-year retrospective of McCardell's designs

1955

Life magazine article features McCardell's designs in fabrics by Picasso, Chagall, Miró, Léger, and Dufy

McCardell featured on the cover of *Time* magazine, the third fashion designer to be so honored

1956

Receives the *Sports Illustrated* American Sportswear Designers Award

Publishes *What Shall I Wear?*

Receives the Parsons School of Design Distinguished Achievement Award for 1956

Receives Editorial Award from *Glamour*

1957

Receives the Lighthouse Award from New York Association for the Blind for helping blind workers demonstrate their skills to the sighted world

1958

Dies on March 22

Inducted into the Coty Hall of Fame

Bibliography

Books

Baker, Patricia. *Fashions of a Decade: The 1950s.* New York: Facts on File, 1991.

———. *Fashions of a Decade: The 1940s.* New York: Facts on File, 1992.

Ballard, Bettina. *In My Fashion: An Intimate Memoir About People, Places, and Events That Make Up the World of High Fashion.* New York: David McKay, 1960.

Berch, Bettina. *Radical by Design: The Life and Style of Elizabeth Hawes, Fashion Designer, Union Organizer, Best Selling Author.* New York: E. P. Dutton, 1988.

Boucher, François. *20,000 Years of Fashion.* New York: Harry N. Abrams, 1967.

Burbank, Emily. *Woman as Decoration.* New York: Dodd, Mead, and Company, 1920.

Candee, Marjorie Dent. *Current Biography.* New York: H. W. Wilson Company, 1942.

Chase, Edna Woolman, and Ilka Chase. *Always in Vogue.* Garden City, N.Y.: Doubleday, 1954.

Costantino, Maria. *Fashions of a Decade. The 1930s.* New York: Facts on File, 1992.

Daves, Jessica. *Ready-Made Miracle.* New York: G. P. Putman's Sons, 1957.

Demornex, Jacqueline. *Madeleine Vionnet.* New York: Rizzoli International Publications, Inc., 1991.

Hawes, Elizabeth. *Fashion is Spinach.* New York: Random House, 1938.

———. *It's Still Spinach.* Boston: Little Brown, 1954.

———. *Why is a Dress?* New York: Viking, 1942.

Head, Edith, and Jane Kesner Admore. *The Dress Doctor.* Boston: Little, Brown, and Company, 1959.

Heal, Edith. *The Young Executive's Wife: You and Your Husband's Job.* New York: Dodd, Mead, 1958.

Horst, Horst P. *Salute to the Thirties.* New York: Viking Press, 1971.

Houck, Catherine. *The Fashion Encyclopedia.* New York: St. Martin's Press, 1982.

Kirke, Betty. *Madeleine Vionnet.* San Francisco: Chronicle Books, 1998.

Lauer, C. Jeanette, and Robert H. Lauer. *Fashion Power.* Upper Saddle River, N.J.: Prentice-Hall, Inc., 1981.

Lee, Sarah Tomerlin, ed. *American Fashion: The Lives and Lines of Adrian, Mainbocher, McCardell, Norrell, Trigère.* New York: Quadrangle, 1975.

Leymarie, Jean. *Chanel.* New York: Rizzoli International Publications, Inc., 1987.

Lyman, Ruth, ed. *Couture.* New York: Doubleday and Company, Inc., 1972.

McCardell, Claire. *What Shall I Wear? The What, Where, When, and How Much of Fashion.* New York: Simon and Schuster, 1956.

———. *Women are What They Wear,* insert in *Sports Illustrated.* New York: Time, Inc., 1954.

Milbank, Caroline Rennolds. *Couture: The Great Designers.* New York: Stewart, Tabori & Chang, 1985.

———. *New York Fashion, The Evolution of American Style.* New York: Harry N. Abrams, 1989.

Raushenbush, Winifred. *How to Dress in Wartime*. Los Angeles: Coward-McCann, Inc., 1942.

Steele, Valerie. *Paris Fashion, A Cultural History*. New York: Oxford University Press, 1981.

————. *Women of Fashion, Twentieth Century Designers*. New York: Rizzoli International Publications, Inc., 1988.

Stegemeyer, Anne. *Who's Who in Fashion*. New York: Fairchild Publications, 1996.

Trahey, Jane, ed. *Harper's Bazaar: 100 Years of the American Female*. New York: Random House, 1967.

Williams, Beryl. *Young Faces in Fashion*. Philadelphia: J. B. Lippincott Company, 1956.

Other

The articles in this section were found in a box of clippings kept by Claire McCardell during her lifetime and by her family after her death. In some cases dates and pages are missing. Often the McCardells did not date the articles they kept. A complete set of these articles can be found in the Archives of the Beneficial-Hodson Library and Technology Center at Hood College in Frederick, Maryland.

"Address of Mr. Stanley Marcus, President, Neiman-Marcus, Dallas & Houston, at the Women's Fashion Group," New York, June 24, 1955.

Callahan, Ellen. "New Bathing Suit Ends Slim Figure Problem." *Daily News* (April 18, 1950).

Cantwell, Mary. "American Style. Claire-voyant." *Mirabella* (September 1994): 50–52.

"Costume Wins Honors for New York Designer." *Women's Wear Daily* (September 7, 1948).

"Couturiere from Frederick." n.p. (n.d.). McCardell Family Archives.

Cozens, Frederick W., and Florence Scovil Stumpf. "Sports in American Life." n.p. (n.d.). McCardell Family Archives.

Dempsey, Margaret. "Maryland Fashions On Fifth Avenue." *Baltimore Sun* (1943, handwritten on article).

Ellicott, Ruth. "Styles for Stay-At-Homes." *Baltimore Sun* (November 2, 1952): A-5.

Elliott, Osburn. "The American Look." *Time* (May 2, 1955): 86–90.

Friedan, Betty. "The gal who defied Dior." *Town Journal* (October 1955).

Gardner, Karen. "Claire McCardell: She founded the women's sportswear movement in American Fashion." *Frederick News-Post* (March 4, 1991): C-1.

Hughes, Alice. "Claire McCardell Wins Rare Honor." n.p. (1955). McCardell Family Archives.

Kehoe, Elena. "A Woman for All Seasons." *Potomac Magazine* (winter 1994–95): 42–45.

Krause, Blanche. "Claire McCardell is Exponent of Younger Look." n.p. (March 6, 1955). McCardell Family Archives.

————. "The Claire McCardell Look." The *Philadelphia Sunday Bulletin* (March 30, 1958).

Lebherz, Richard. "In the Claire McCardell Corner." *Frederick News-Post* (November 11, 1971).

LeBoutillier, Peg. "The Cult of Claire McCardell" (unpublished, n.d.). McCardell Family Archives.

Maryland Women's Hall of Fame. Program from the 1991 Induction Ceremony. Annapolis: Maryland Commission on Women, March 5, 1991.

McCardell, Claire. "Speech to Young People Graduating from Design School." (n.d.). McCardell Family Archives.

————. "Two Fashions for the 'Girl on the Job'." n.p. (n.d.). McCardell Family Archives.

———. Untitled speech given when presented with the Coty Award, February 1944.

———. "Wardrobe Futures." *Washington Star* (February 9, 1945).

Morris, Bernadine. "A Chronicle of Sportswear." *New York Times* (April 5, 1985).

———. "Remembering Claire McCardell." *New York Times* section 2 (February 2, 1981): 42.

Parnell, Dorothy. "Have You Heard?" *Milwaukee Sentinel* (March 26, 1958).

Richards, Alice. "Designer Creates With Ideas Not Pencil." *Atlanta Journal* (September 7, 1950).

Robb, Inez. "Designer Advocates What Many Practice." *Clarion Ledger,* Jackson, Miss. (April 19, 1953): 2.

Rousuck, J. Wynn. "McCardell fashions earned their survival." *Baltimore Sun* (May 16, 1976).

Scarborough, Katherine. "Couturiere from Frederick." n.p. (1946). McCardell Family Archives.

Sheppard, Eugenia. "Team of McCardell and Klein Turned the Tide of U.S. Fashion." *Baltimore News American* (August 23, 1968).

Simpson, Gay. "Prophetic Fashions Average High Score at Neiman Shows." n.p. (n.d.). McCardell Family Archives.

"Six Women Receive Press Group Honors." *Washington Post* (April 16, 1950): 12M.

"Sophisticated Slouch Keynote of Designer's Fall Fashions." n.p. (n.d.). McCardell Family Archives.

"Sports Clothes Changed our Lives." Press release. n.p. (n.d.). McCardell Family Archives.

"Taking a Second Look at Claire McCardell." n.p. (n.d.). McCardell Family Archives.

"Three Designers Win Awards As 'Tops in Their Field in 1943'." n.p. (n.d.). McCardell Family Archives.

Tracy, Virginia. "Capezio Creates Memorial Tribute to Maryland's Claire McCardell." *Baltimore-American* (August 30, 1959).

Tucker, Priscilla. "The Name Behind the Names." *Herald Tribune* (October 16, 1961).

"Wearers of her designs toast McCardell's Memory." *The Baltimore Sun* (February 29, 1981).

Whalen, Grover. Letter to Eleanore McCardell. October 3, 1958.

"Who's News and Why." n.p. (November 1954). McCardell Family Archives.

"Women's National Press Club Will Honor Claire McCardell." n.p. (April 7, 1950). McCardell Family Archives.

Wulbern, Helen. "Designers of Today and Tomorrow." *Women's Wear Daily* (November 14, 1940): 4.

Index

Photograph Credits

The authors and publisher gratefully acknowledge the photographers, companies, publications, museums, and individuals listed below for supplying the necessary materials and permission to reproduce their work. Special thanks to the McCardell family, who were so generous with their archives. Those credits not listed in the captions are provided below. References are to page numbers.

14, 15 (all pictures), 17, 18 (above and below), 19 (left and right), 22, 24 (below), 25, 34 (above), 36, 41, 43, 47, 50, 56, 67, 71, 72, 99, 102, 107 (below), 115 (above), 119, 120 (left), 131, 136: Courtesy McCardell Family Archives

11: Courtesy Photoresearchers, Inc.; 24 (above): Courtesy Horst Studios; 34 (below): Courtesy Nordiska Museet; 35: Copyright © 1950 Center for Creative Photography, Arizona Board of Regents; 38: Copyright © 1945 (renewed 1973) by the Condé Nast Publications Inc.; 39: Copyright © 1938 Center for Creative Photography, Arizona Board of Regents; 44: Copyright © 1939 (renewed 1967, 1995) by the Condé Nast Publications Inc.; 51: Copyright © 1942 Center for Creative Photography, Arizona Board of Regents; 53: Copyright © 1950 (renewed 1978) by the Condé Nast Publications, Inc.; 54: Copyright © 1944 (renewed 1972) by the Condé Nast Publications, Inc.; 55: Copyright © 1947 Center for Creative Photography, Arizona Board of Regents; 59: Copyright © 1943 Center for Creative Photography, Arizona Board of Regents; 61: Courtesy Brooklyn Museum of Art. Libraries. Special Collections; 62: Copyright © 1941 (renewed 1969, 1997) by the Condé Nast Publications, Inc.; 66: Courtesy Brooklyn Museum of Art. Libraries. Special Collections; 68: Copyright © Time Inc. Reprinted with permission; 75: Copyright © 1953 (renewed 1974) by the Condé Nast Publications, Inc.; 77: Copyright © 1946 (renewed 1974) by the Condé Nast Publications, Inc.; 80: Copyright © 1953 (renewed 1974) by the Condé Nast Publications, Inc.; 81: Courtesy The Anna-Maria and Stephen Kellen Archives of Parsons School of Design; 83: Copyright © 1947 Center for Creative Photography, Arizona Board of Regents; 86: Courtesy Horst Studios; 87: Reproduced from Marcel Rochas. *Vingt-cinq ans d'élégance* (Paris: 1951); 90: Copyright © 1945 Center for Creative Photography, Arizona Board of Regents; 91: Copyright © 1944 (renewed 1972) by the Condé Nast Publications, Inc.; 92: Courtesy Christa Zinner; 93: Courtesy Staley-Wise Gallery, New York; 94: Copyright © 1941 (renewed 1969, 1997) by the Condé Nast Publications, Inc.; 105: Courtesy Time, Inc. Copyright © 1955. Reprinted by permission; 106: Copyright © 1943 Center for Creative Photography, Arizona Board of Regents; 107 (above): Courtesy Sidney Frissel Stafford; 108: Courtesy Avedon Studios; 110: Copyright © 1953 Center for Creative Photography, Arizona Board of Regents; 111: Copyright © 1958 Center for Creative Photography, Arizona Board of Regents; 114: Copyright © 1958 (renewed 1986) by the Condé Nast Publications, Inc.; 115 (below): Courtesy the authors; 118: Copyright © 1945 (renewed 1973) by the Condé Nast Publications, Inc.; 121: Courtesy Photoresearchers, Inc.; 126: Courtesy Historical Society of Frederick County, Maryland; 127 (above): Copyright © *Washington Post*. Reprinted with permission of the District of Columbia Public Library; 128: Courtesy Photoresearchers, Inc.; 129: Courtesy Photoresearchers, Inc.